8.00

ARTIST IN IOWA

GRANT WOOD

ARTIST
in IOWA

A life of

GRANT WOOD

By DARRELL GARWOOD

W · W · NORTON & COMPANY · INC · New York

To Helen

Foreword

My INTEREST in Grant Wood goes back to 1934 when, as a student at the University of Iowa, I wrote a feature story for an Iowa newspaper in which I hailed him as the leader of a new liberal wing on the art faculty. During the succeeding years I continued to follow the events of his career and to assemble notes about him and his work. It was not until after his death, however, that the present biography was undertaken and it has been made possible chiefly because of assistance received from people in Cedar Rapids.

While I was in that city gathering material I spent much time with Mr. David Turner, who not only provided me with everything possible from his own recollections and records but put me in touch with many others who had been important in the artist's life. It was Mr. Turner who introduced me to Miss Frances Prescott, principal of the high school where Grant Wood taught, and to Marvin Cone, his lifelong friend. And it was with Mr. Turner that I first went to the home of Paul and Vida Hanson, whose loyal friendship meant so much to Grant. I saw John Reid, who opened his files and spent many hours recalling everything he could that would be of help. I visited Henry S. Ely, who took me to Stone City. I later met the artist's sister Mrs. Nan Wood Graham in Los Angeles, and his brother Frank Wood in Waterloo, Iowa. I was surprised to find the Wood family history documented back to 1725. There is very little of this in the book, as many readers would not want to pause long in contemplation of a family tree; but if more information is desired as to why the Woods left spacious homes

7

in the east to pioneer in the west, Frank Wood has it down to the last detail.

To all those mentioned in this foreword, and to nearly everyone mentioned in the book, I am indebted for information. I am also indebted to Darrel McConkey and Frank Severance for technical help with the manuscript, and to Harry Boyd who read the work in proof.

The illustrations in this book have been selected as representative of Grant Wood's work. Grateful acknowledgment is made to Van Vechten Shaffer, Joslyn Memorial, Chicago Art Institute, Edward G. Robinson, King Vidor, Whitney Museum of American Art, Jo Hennessey, Abbott Laboratories, who have given permission for the reproduction of the paintings in their possession.

DARRELL GARWOOD

Silver Spring, Maryland

Contents

CONTENTS

Illustrations

Honor at Home

GRANT WOOD came to Cedar Rapids, Iowa, as a square-faced boy
of ten. His mother had just been widowed, had sold the family
farm, and had used a good part of the money to buy a two-story
frame house on Northeast Fourteenth Street for herself and her
four children, Frank, Grant, Jack and Nan. Even then Grant
could draw very neat and sometimes funny pictures on the side-
walks and on the walls of buildings, but he didn't attract much
attention at first.

Gradually as he grew older people became aware that a great
artist, or at least an artist, was in their midst. He was accepted
as something of which the city could be proud. Well-to-do families hired him to help decorate their homes. Friends found work
for him and looked after his interests when they could.

David Turner, a funeral director, gave him a hayloft in which
to live and paint free of rent, and exhibited his pictures in the
Turner Funeral Home. Turner also persuaded people to buy
Grant's paintings, and generally undertook to keep his affairs in
order, which wasn't always an easy task.

On one occasion, in 1925, they had gone to the capital at Des
Moines to help decorate the newly completed Dunn Funeral
Home. At that time Grant made more money as an interior decorator than as a painter. Turner had spread his name among
funeral directors and his advice was in demand. He was engaged
in hanging one of his paintings in the Dunn Home, and stood in
front of it with a hammer in his hand.

He was short and stout and wore a brown, thickly woven suit.
His head was large and his hair a reddish-brown color. He wore

heavy glasses, his cheekbones were high, and he was inclined to squint. His chin jutted and was deeply cleft. The most peculiar thing about him was that he never stood still but swayed from side to side, resting his weight first on one foot and then the other.

He stood there swaying now, studying the picture long after he must have seen everything there was to see. Then he looked at his wrist watch and glanced at Dave Turner. He walked the full length of the room to lay the hammer on a bench, walked back to where Turner was standing, and said calmly: "I just remembered that I have an appointment with Mrs. Douglas in Cedar Rapids. I'll have to leave."

After a pause to let Dave think that over, the artist added: "The train is leaving in fifteen minutes."

David Turner, big, active and accustomed to dealing with complicated situations, sized up this one quickly: if the appointment was with Mrs. Douglas, it was important—she was one of the wealthiest women in Cedar Rapids; fifteen minutes might be just time enough to get Grant through two miles of traffic to the railroad station.

So he grabbed his overcoat and hat, dogtrotted to his automobile, and had the motor racing by the time Grant got there. As they swung down Grand Avenue, Grant remarked: "My clothes are at the Des Moines club."

Dave stepped on the gas. It meant more driving through traffic and a stop at the Des Moines club, but he still thought he would make the train. He pulled up in front of the club door and waited while Grant went for his clothes.

The artist had taken off his overcoat and was actually hurrying a little when he came back with his suitcase. But as he dropped into the front seat he said: "I haven't got any money."

Grant Wood was extremely deliberate in his speech, even when pressed by events. He spoke like a schoolboy reading in a bad light, with pauses so that the listener had constantly to pick up his words and string them into sentences.

"I haven't—got—any—money," was the way this news came to Dave, like something relayed to him on a telegraph wire. He turned around to give Grant a hopeless look, and then went into action. He had only a few dollars himself, so he ran into the nearest restaurant and planted himself in front of the proprietor.

"I'm David Turner. I run a mortuary in Cedar Rapids and I've got to have twenty-five dollars at once. Will you give it to me?"

The proprietor had never heard of David Turner and wasn't interested in mortuaries or Cedar Rapids, but he did a strange thing. After staring blankly for a moment, he reached into the cash register, pulled out twenty-five dollars, and, with no more security than a "much obliged" thrown over Dave's shoulder, saw the money out the door.

Turner managed to get Grant onto the train as it was pulling out, and came back to his car flushed but feeling that a difficult job had been well done. His face fell when he opened the car door. It was bitter cold, but Grant had forgotten his overcoat. In a pocket of the coat were his heavy glasses, without which he couldn't see much farther than a mole.

Such lapses never persuaded the people of Cedar Rapids that Grant Wood was anything less than a genuine artist. It is true there were few who foresaw his later fame, but people felt that he was at least touched with genius, and if he couldn't remember names or appointments, if he swayed from side to side, wore a vacant expression, didn't know what became of his money, or doggedly insisted on something that didn't make sense—that only went to prove it.

No criticism of Grant or his art ever went unanswered in Cedar Rapids. Even his satirical *Daughters of Revolution* received lavish praise in the conservative Cedar Rapids *Gazette*, and long articles were devoted to cracking the skulls of critics who wrote captiously about *American Gothic* or *Woman with Plants*. More than four hundred of his paintings hang on the various walls of Cedar Rapids, and most of them were bought before the outside world even began to recognize him. He was not without honor in his home town.

A family legend that he would be an artist started when he was two years old. The Woods had gone for dinner to the home of his mother's young cousin, Clarabelle Weaver. Mrs. Wood had put Grant into a new black-silk dress and was hoping to show him off to his best advantage, but she was sadly disappointed. He bawled and kicked and swung his fists every time anyone tried to take him from his mother, and even she could hardly keep him quiet.

So it happened that when everyone else had finished a farm-sized meal, Mrs. Wood hadn't yet had a chance to eat. Clarabelle stepped into the situation, took Grant firmly under the arms and despite his kicking and screaming proceeded to walk back and forth across the room with him. She was soon gratified as Grant became silent. Then she noticed that he appeared to be gazing at the pictures on the walls.

It is possible that Grant was only out of breath, but Clarabelle preferred to believe that he was awed into silence by the pictures, some of which were her own—she did a little painting, as did many other young ladies of that time. She called attention to his fixed interest in the pictures, and predicted he would grow up to be an artist.

Only a year later, when Grant was three, his mother found him with a pencil making clusters of tiny arcs, all opening in the same direction and looking like so many half-moons or fingernail cuttings. They didn't mean anything to Mrs. Wood until he told her he was making a picture of a chicken. She decided that made sense: she had some Plymouth Rock hens, and half-moons would be the proper thing to describe their wavy, black-and-white markings. Mrs. Wood had taught primary grades at Anamosa, Iowa, before her marriage, and she knew how to talk to a child. She told him it was a nice picture.

When he was four, Grant chose a wintry day to follow his older brother Frank to Antioch Country School, which stands next to red-brick Antioch Church on Highway No. 64, three and a half miles southeast of Anamosa. The school could be reached by cutting down through a ravine on the Wood farm. Grant was a stubborn child, and he trudged along through the snow behind Frank even though his brother turned around repeatedly and told him to go home. Whenever Frank stopped, Grant stopped; when Frank went on, Grant followed along.

Frank reached the school; Grant was twenty or thirty yards behind him. Grant saw the other children around the school and was afraid to come any farther, but he still wouldn't go back. He stood there in the path while Frank, who was eight, shouted at him to go home. Older boys joined in the shouting. Then they threw snowballs. Some of the snowballs hit Grant, and he began to cry, but he still stood there. Finally his mother came down through the ravine and took him home.

That adventure was interpreted as showing an unusual thirst for knowledge, fully in line with his artistic ability. Had Grant only known it, there wasn't much art being taught at Antioch School. He found that out later, and never took much interest in his school work except when he could relate it to drawing or painting in some extracurricular way. For the time being, he contented himself with drawing chickens.

He never tired of the chickens. He drew houses, barns, trees, cows and cats, but mostly he drew chickens. He could make a very good likeness of a chicken long before he reached Cedar Rapids, and he drew them on all occasions—roosters crowing, roosters fighting, hens on eggs, hens wishing they were on eggs, hostile hens, friendly hens, indifferent hens.

Those chickens are now immortal. They cluck about the barnyard in *Dinner for Threshers*. They scowl and peer in *Adolescence*. They strut across the immaculate lawn of *Herbert Hoover's Birthplace*, and one of them gazes at the world from *The Appraisal*. Grant tried loyally to get them into *Stone City*. He cut little chickens out of paper and held them here and there on the painting to see how they would fit in, but finally decided they would spoil his design.

Grant drew the chickens because he liked them. But as a boy he of course heard the talk of his elders that he would grow up to be an artist, and that may be why he pursued his drawing with such single-minded purpose. Perhaps, too, that is why he added a flourish, a historic touch when at the age of eight he lettered his name with a pencil in the dank and murky cellar of their farm home.

His inscription, still dimly legible on a stone and concrete support under the staring old farmhouse, reads:

GRANT WOOD WAS BORN HERE, FEB. 13, 1891

Father and Son

THE Woods came west from Winchester, Virginia. Grant's great-grandfather was Jesse Wood, a Quaker merchant who lived in the high-porched Winchester home which eventually came to be occupied by Harry K. Thaw, of headline fame. Jesse's brother David and his sister Thirissa were already in Ohio on January 22, 1832, when Thirissa wrote from "Woodland, Urbana, Ohio" urging him to "sell and come out here." "It is a wild-looking place yet and the inhabitants have scarcely become civilized yet," she admitted. "They wear linsy hunting shirts and blanket coats and every day is alike to them. They know no Sabbath but are as independent a set of Devils as ever lived. (There's not a lawyer in Winchester knows more than they do.)" On the other hand she assured him that "All that appears to be wanting is society," and "There is a place near here that would suit thee, a beautiful piece of land and well watered."

Jesse stayed on in Winchester and died there, but his only son Joseph followed Thirissa's advice and went west twenty-seven years later. Winchester hadn't developed commercially on the scale of its early promise, and as Quakers the Woods were opposed to slavery—Joseph Wood left Virginia with his wife Rebecca Shepherd in 1859, the year John Brown and his friends were hanged for storming the arsenal at Harpers Ferry. After five years in Illinois, Joseph and Rebecca boarded a steam train and moved into Iowa. They rode to the railhead at Clinton, on the Mississippi River, then bought a team of horses and drove in a buckboard wagon across the prairie to Anamosa, sixty-five miles farther on. They picked out a circular swell of land, set out maple,

19

evergreen and pine trees, built a large frame house and outbuildings and called it Circle Farm. One of their children was Francis Maryville Wood, Grant Wood's father, who was always called Maryville (Mur-vil).

Like Grant, the father was square-faced and blond, and he had a somewhat startled expression in his youth. He was registered for two years at Lennox College in Hopkinton, Iowa, where his principal interest was history. After leaving the college he worked five years on his father's farm. Then, in 1879, he bought an eighty-acre place nearby for $1,850 and for the next seven years farmed on both his own and his father's land.

He had known Hattie Weaver since childhood, but apparently didn't begin to think of marriage until his late twenties—he was the only one of Joseph's five children to marry at all. Hattie's people, the Weavers, had taken up land west of Anamosa the same year that the Woods settled southeast of the town. The two families differed on politics—the Woods were Republicans from Virginia; the Weavers were Democrats from upstate New York—but their paths crossed frequently in other respects. Joseph Wood didn't find many Quakers in his neighborhood, so he joined the Presbyterian church at Anamosa; the Weavers were already Presbyterian, and went to the same church. The Woods and the Weavers bought adjacent family cemetery lots in Riverside Cemetery at Anamosa.

On January 6, 1886, Maryville and Hattie were married. He was thirty; she was twenty-eight. Maryville added two small lots to his farm and bought forty-four acres of timber at some distance for fuel. Hattie had been teaching at Strawberry Hill School in Anamosa, and had saved her money. She bought most of their furniture. She got twelve dining chairs, and that wasn't always enough when the Wood and Weaver families were together. It was a day of plush albums, kerosene lamps, plenty to eat and much hospitality.

There was no thought of hardship on the farm. The Woods had everything necessary to life; they lived as well as the average family of the time. Hattie was a plain, home person, who wasn't any hand to assert herself or stir up a fuss, and she and Maryville got on well together. Their children were born over a period of thirteen years, Frank at the end of the first year, Grant in 1891, Jack in 1893 and Nan in 1899. These were the last children to be born to the Iowa branch of the Wood family tree.

The two-story farmhouse stood among a few trees on an otherwise bare rise in the ground. A dirt road led between fence posts up to it, and as visitors came closer they could see the farm buildings lower down behind the house. There was a board fence between the house yard and the barnyard. As a small, fair-haired boy, Grant used to sit on that fence, watching the chickens and turkeys and waiting for his father to bring the horses out of the barn. He would hear the clank of the harness, and then the horses would appear one at a time, his father behind them. Grant would wait until the horses had stepped into their places before a corn-plow or rake and his father had driven off to the field. Then he would go back to the kitchen, move toward the nickel-ornamented kitchen range, lift a lid and begin examining the remains of the breakfast fire.

Mrs. Wood knew what he was after. Sometimes, if the fire were still burning, she would reach in and pull out a partly burned stick for him; sometimes she would have saved one for him in the woodbox. Grant would take the charred stick and a square of cardboard from a box of crackers, or a sheet of brown wrapping paper. These were his drawing materials. His brother Frank was often down at the barn, or working in the family garden or even in the field. His younger brother Jack and later his infant sister Nan were around the house, but he got privacy by crawling under the oval dining-room table. The table was covered with a red-checkered cloth, the points of which hung nearly to the floor; the space inside with its arched openings was Grant's first studio.

He might work most of a day over his charcoal drawings. On other days, he might wander along the dusty roads of the neighborhood and down by the Wapsipinicon River, the Wapsie. He used to sit by the Wapsie and imagine that some day he would build a raft like Huckleberry Finn's and float down to the Mississippi. He explored as far as the hills and limestone quarries of Stone City, eight miles away. One of his big boyhood projects was a list of birds and their habits. He sent the list of birds and a hand-lettered article on the subject to the weekly newspaper at Anamosa. The editor boiled the matter down to one paragraph, and eventually, on April 15, 1901, the Anamosa *Eureka* published this item:

Master Grant Wood, only ten years of age, reports that he has found 55 varieties of birds in this neighborhood. His communication on this subject is very interesting and shows that he is an observing, thoughtful, wide-awake boy.

No doubt Maryville looked at Grant now and then and wondered how he had happened to bring such a son into the world. The father liked masculine qualities, and regarded history, science, hard work and the proper exercise of authority as masculine; religion, art and light fiction as somehow feminine. Yet he raised no particular objection to Grant's drawing, and said little when the talk went around about his son's becoming an artist. What did exasperate him about Grant was his failure to mind promptly. When Grant was interested in something, he wasn't inclined to leave it, or even to hear what he was told. His father insisted on prompt obedience. They clashed frequently on this issue.

Maryville had been brought up in a school of strict discipline, and he tried to keep the tradition going, with willow switches. There was a treeful of such switches in the yard, and he used them several times on Grant. These were serious occasions in the Wood family. Hattie would become very tense and busy over her stove. The father would be upset and would retire into a glum silence to read a biography of Abraham Lincoln, Macaulay's *History of England,* or *The Decline and Fall of the Roman Empire.* Sometimes, after things had quieted down, he read snatches of these out loud.

He decided that Cooper was more suitable for the children, and read all of *The Deerslayer* and *The Last of the Mohicans* out loud. He also read them Dickens' *Child's History of England,* and a number of other books which he thought worthwhile. But when his sister Sarah brought a copy of *Grimm's Fairy Tales* from Grandmother Wood's place a half mile away, Maryville refused to let the children have it. "This is too foolish to be reading; it's a waste of time," he declared, after looking into the fairy tales, and he returned the book unread. He was a member of the Presbyterian church, but he didn't go in for Bible reading much, and didn't have any family prayers—not even the customary mumbled prayers before meals. He went to town frequently, liked to talk politics and didn't mind spending money for a new book if one of the proper weight came out.

In the fall of 1900, Maryville became ill. He was short of breath; he thought he was suffering from asthma. He kept to his bed most of the winter of 1900–1. The farm work fell on Frank, who was fourteen, and Grant tried to help him. They milked several cows, fed the hogs and broke the ice on the watering tank. Every so often they hitched a team to a sled, covered themselves with a buffalo robe, and went to the timber lot for fuel. Mrs. Wood thought this very dangerous and spent anxious hours fearing the horses would run away, but nothing of the sort ever happened.

Maryville's condition seemed to improve. One day he got up, said he felt much better, was sure he was going to be all right and thought he would go to town that day. He began moving about the house. Before he could get started for town, he collapsed, and died a few hours later. That was on March 11, 1901; he was forty-five years old. People said he died of heart failure, and the doctor couldn't come any closer to the cause.

The pioneers were posterity minded, and Maryville Wood more than most had looked into the past and the future. But the possibility of his early death was something he hadn't considered, nor could he foresee that the family's name would survive only on paintings. The plans he had made for his children had to be changed, and none of them became farmers. Grant's days of sitting on the barnyard fence were over.

THREE

Neighborhood Cowboy

It was decided that Mrs. Wood should go with her children to Cedar Rapids, thirty miles to the southwest, where her father DeVolson Weaver was living in retirement. The farm, livestock and machinery were sold, and the place on Northeast Fourteenth Street was bought—these matters were arranged by her brother Frank Weaver, a fine, scholarly-looking gentleman who had served Omaha as city attorney and who was known as Judge Weaver on his visits to Iowa. Several months were consumed in transactions; when Mrs. Wood finally got her goods and her children into the bare two-story house that was her own, she felt as though she never wanted to leave it.

And she seldom did during the next fifteen years; she stayed very close to home. Her widowhood seemed to involve a lower social status, and she had to get along on as little money as possible. Maryville's estate had amounted to about $5,000, and she had spent $2,550 for the house and lot. She made the rest of the money go a long way.

The Wood home, an upright structure with a full-length porch, sat forward on one corner of the lot, immediately beside an alley. The remainder of the block on its right was vacant, down to C Avenue. Across the alley to the left was a stable, occupied by a driving horse, and beyond that with its back turned to face on B Avenue was the home of Mary and Anna Woitishek, maiden sisters, and their elderly father, owner of the horse. The Woitisheks had farm and city property and were well-to-do. Mrs. Wood never ventured to pay them a visit. She did invite them over one day to meet her brother Judge Weaver. Anna, the younger of the

25

sisters, and her father came and shook his hand. That was the only time the two families met socially.

Frank and Grant, however, went to the Woitisheks, mowed their lawn and did other odd jobs about the place. Grant for some time looked after the horse of Dr. Richard Lord up the street. Mrs. Wood saw to it that their back yard was put into garden every year, and sometimes Grant went about selling tomatoes, string beans or corn when they had more than his mother wanted to can. He also got some work bringing in and milking a cow or two for different neighbors. It was common at that time for families living well out in Cedar Rapids to keep a cow, since pasturage could be had within a few blocks. Grant was a "neighborhood cowboy," like many other youths of his age. Even sons of well-off families did this kind of choring to pick up spending money.

Mrs. Wood wasn't considered exactly poor. The expression for it was that she didn't have much to do with. But she was a householder and her father was a man of some means, ready to help out in the early years. Frank was almost fifteen when they moved into the house; when he was seventeen, Grandfather Weaver undertook to start him in the automobile business. It had been customary on the farm to present a son with a team of horses when he got big enough to do a day's work; considering the times, Grandfather Weaver did the next best thing: he bought Frank a "one-lung" Cadillac which, with its high seats and guy wires holding down the top, was the marvel of the neighborhood.

Grant was not as impressed by the Cadillac as might be supposed. He liked to do "fiddlely" things, to draw, to paint and to make gadgets that would work, and on these matters his concentration was intense. But he never became much of a motorist—his mind would wander and the cars wandered with it. While Frank was trying out his Cadillac, Grant was practicing his drawing with a neighbor girl, Annette Brown. He and Annette were in the eighth grade; they entered drawings in a contest conducted by a national crayon company; both won first prizes—three first prizes were awarded in Cedar Rapids. Grant's drawing was a study of a cluster of oak leaves, and the prize was his first formal artistic recognition.

By this time Grant was finding various means to connect art with his school work. When they studied Wordsworth's poem about the daffodils under Miss Robina Wilson, he brought her a water color of English daffodils bending to the breeze, and when they studied Longfellow's poem about the ship of state he painted her a ship at sea. He also drew her the head of a chicken and made her a book cover. Despite such dealings with teachers, which might have gotten him a reputation as a sissy, he was seldom called names; even then there seems to have been a certain respect for his ability.

Besides it was a serious matter to arouse him. He wasn't especially muscular, and several times got the worst of it in fights, but he was persistent in both his likes and dislikes and he had a deep, lasting anger. His brother Jack would fly into fits of rage and swing his fists about, then be the finest fellow in the world a few minutes later. His brother Frank was inclined to take the sensible view, to shake hands and to forget unpleasant matters. Grant, however, seldom forgot an offense. Even when beaten in a fight, he would get up as red and defiant as when he started. Under extreme pressure he might shake hands but there would still be a chill between him and his late antagonist. It wasn't any fun to torment him.

During one summer between school terms Grant decided to work on a farm. His companion on this venture was Larry Bartlett, the son of a contractor. They took their case to Anna Woitishek, who asked a tenant on one of the Woitishek farms if Grant and Larry could come out there for the summer. The tenant, a Dane named Jorgenson, replied that he didn't have any place for them to sleep. Anna reported this to Grant.

27

"That's all right; we'll sleep in the haymow."

"It wouldn't be very healthy for you, sleeping on that damp hay."

"We'll take a blanket."

Anna reopened negotiations, and Jorgenson agreed to take them provided they slept in the barn. "Don't work these boys very hard; they aren't used to it," Anna told him. Grant and Larry stuck it out in the haymow for three weeks. They helped Jorgenson around the barn and a little in the field. That was as near as Grant ever came to doing actual farm work.

"How did you like the farm?" Anna asked him when he had returned home.

"It was all right; only the rats ran over us when we were asleep."

From the time he entered Washington High School, one of Grant's closest friends was Marvin Cone. He and Marvin were the staff artists for everything that needed staff artists, and were in charge of the stage properties and decorations for whatever was going on. They built a stockade and a blockhouse, a cottage and a section of the *Mayflower* for a showing of *Priscilla*, painted scenery for various other plays and made drawings for the school magazine and annual. They also worked with the Cedar Rapids Art Association, which had a gallery over the public library. Grant got a cot and slept in the gallery part of the time to save the cost of a watchman. When exhibits were given he and Marvin unpacked the pictures. Artists had a habit of gluing heavy paper over the glass on their pictures so that if it were broken, pieces of the glass wouldn't damage the painting, and Grant and Marvin spent hours scraping the stuff off with razor blades.

One of their projects was an attempt to make reliefs of each other by pouring plaster over their faces, using soda straws to breathe through. It wasn't a success. They nearly suffocated, and a chunk of Grant's hair had to be pulled out before the plaster could be removed. Grant later improved his technique, and made some successful reliefs by this method.

He got his first money for painting from Mrs. John H. Barry. The Barrys lived on B Avenue at Eighth Street and had a metal shop in the basement for their sons. Grant was doing some work in metals with them and needed eight dollars for materials. He approached Mrs. Barry with a painting of a bluff and some gnarled trees, reflected in water, which he had done at nearby Palisades Park.

"How much do you think the painting is worth?" Mrs. Barry asked.

"It isn't worth much, but I need eight dollars."

They agreed on that price. Grant also made some money designing bookplates; the Woitisheks gave him fifteen dollars for one of these. He had enough money to buy the materials for a course in design which was running serially in a magazine called the *Craftsman*. The *Craftsman* lessons were written by Ernest Batchelder, who had been an instructor at the Harvard University Summer School of Design, and Grant studied them religiously. Following Batchelder's instructions he bought a drawing board, squared underlaid and engine-ruled paper, transparent water-color paper, water colors, large and small brushes and India ink, and would be waiting at the newsstand when the issues of the *Craftsman* came out.

His high-school grades were erratic, ranging from 70 to 89 in algebra, 70 to 91 in geometry, 63 to 85 in English history, and 74 to 87 in Greek history. There wasn't much range in his grades in Roman history and civics, which came out 75, 75, 73 and 76, 75, 75. He started with a 75, worked up to an 88 and fell to a 79 in chemistry, and did fairly well in zoology (86, 87, 81) and botany (80, 89, 86). There wasn't any art on the curriculum. He had a steady 95 in manual training.

One of his most humiliating experiences in high school came

when a teacher held one of his water colors under a faucet to blur the lines. Grant was inclined toward solid lines in painting, as in drawing, whereas the prevailing artistic mode called for broken lines and emphasis on the blurring effect of the atmosphere. The teacher tried to explain this to him, and to improve the picture by running water over it.

When they graduated in 1910, Grant and Marvin as usual were in charge of the decorations and seating arrangements. They didn't want to sit conspicuously in the front row, but they wanted to be able to get their diplomas without leaving their places. So they took seats in the second row and arranged the speaker's rostrum so they would be able to reach over the front row for their sheepskins. This saved them the major embarrassment of walking down an aisle before a houseful of indulgent parents.

That same night, after the graduation exercises, Grant took a train for Minneapolis. He didn't know anyone in Minneapolis, but Ernest Batchelder was scheduled to teach that summer at the Minneapolis School of Design and Handicraft and Normal Art, generally called the Handicraft Guild. While pondering over the lessons in the *Craftsman* he had acquired a great admiration for Batchelder, and he meant to study under him.

Grant was often unsure of himself. Even in high school he had the habit of swaying from side to side, and he frequently ran a finger uneasily through the deep cleft in his chin. But he was feeling confident that night, and his high cheekbones were colored. His reddish-blond hair, which he used to call pink, was combed in a heavy shock to the right, and he wore a stiff collar, a black bow tie, and his graduation suit. He smiled when Marvin protested that he should wait a while.

Marvin, a little dazed by the sudden departure, saw him off at the train. He figured Grant didn't have more than thirty or forty dollars, and he marveled at his courage.

Hanson & Wood

OF ALL the haphazard schooling Grant got during the next four-teen years, that first summer in Minneapolis was the best. Everything, as he saw it, worked out well for him. The young man who stepped off the train was a slender youth of nineteen who looked even younger. He wore a cap, and his head was held back by a high stiff collar. He walked to the Handicraft Guild, which was located on Tenth Street between Nicollet and Marquette avenues.

He said he didn't have much money. That didn't make any difference, he was told; he could work his way in the school's shop. Could he study under Batchelder? Certainly, everyone would study under Batchelder that summer. Could they tell him where to get a room? Yes, and they would find a roommate.

His roommate was Harold Kelly, also a student. They paid rent for a while, and then decided that if they could save rent money they would have enough to buy new fall suits of clothes. They got jobs that provided them sleeping space in a mortuary, but the jobs didn't last long. Grant liked to tell a story about why they left the mortuary.

"We had to help carry the cadavers down a flight of stairs to the chapel," he would say. "One night we were carrying down an old gentleman and his toupee kept slipping off. The fellow we were working for got a hammer and some tacks and tacked it on. That was too much for us."

The story, however, is a joke hoary with age among morticians, and chances are that Grant adapted it to himself. Actually, the mortician complained, he wanted the boys around to answer telephones in the evening and often they didn't get in until midnight or later. They weren't satisfied either; the cots they were given were separated from the embalming room only by a thin partition, and they didn't like the odors that floated around them.

They thought they would rather sleep in a park—and that is what they did. It was before the police everywhere had accepted the idea that spending the night in a public place was a crime, and they got some solid hours of sleep on the benches at Loring Park. The noise of motorcars speeding down Harmon Place bothered them for a while, but they got used to it. When it rained, they knew an all-night restaurant where they could sit and drink coffee until the weather cleared.

To Grant making jewelry and decorative items in the school's shop could hardly be considered work—he had been doing things like that for the fun of it, and now he had a proper forge and tools. Because of his experience in the Barrys' shop, he was far ahead of most of the students, and his work drew quick praise. He foresaw for himself a possible career as a metalworker.

Above all, he achieved his ambition to study under Batchelder. Then well known throughout the country, Batchelder already had such stature in Grant's mind that he might easily have proved a disappointment. The fact was that he lived up to every expectation. The teacher who washed the water color under the faucet would have had little sympathy from Batchelder, a craftsman and a designer who thought there was nobility in a good strong line. He knew how to bend those lines into living shapes, how to emphasize an idea, how to make the trees bow and the earth billow.

Some of this ability, especially the billowing earth, was already apparent in Grant's painting: that roll of the ground which was one of the chief things to attract comment in his later landscapes can be seen in water colors he painted as early as 1905, when he was entering high school. Batchelder liked Grant's work, and gave him more than usual attention. In later years, Grant considered it the most important instruction of his life.

32

It was at Minneapolis, too, that he first acquired the feeling for Gothic architecture. Batchelder spoke of the Gothic period as "those bygone days when art was not afraid of the grime and soot, the din and clatter of the workshop," and summed up what seemed to him one of the period's most satisfactory virtues by adding: "There were no artists then; nothing but craftsmen— some better than others." It was a revival of "the spirit that built the cathedrals of France" that Batchelder sought for American art.

At the end of the summer Grant returned to Cedar Rapids to find his uncle Clarence Wood determined that he should become a mechanic. Uncle Clarence thought it was time he settled down to steady work. Under pressure, Grant took a job as a machinist's assistant at the Rock Island railroad shops, but he didn't last long at it. He said he wasn't going to spend his time just turning a wheel. The fact was that he had no inclination for what was called regular work, and couldn't apply himself to it. He could work only at what interested him, and this included painting, metalworking and decorating. Nothing was too much trouble if it happened to appeal to him. He stayed up all one night to finish decorating a gocart for a little girl named Dorothy Bowser, and with it she won a prize in a parade contest. An effort like this, that would please someone, always attracted him more than money. He developed a technique for making plaster flowers, which he cast in a glue mold and then painted—he called them glue flowers. These flowers didn't last, and were worth nothing at all, but he enjoyed giving them to people. In another profitless venture, he mixed whites of eggs, juices and strained honey with barn paint, trying to find the secret of how the old masters had mixed their translucent paints. He did earn a little money by working in the metal shop of Mrs. Charles ("Kate") Loomis. They made rings, pins, necklaces, lamps and novelties and sold them for what they could get.

Among the ideas he was turning over in his head was that he might become an illustrator. He mentioned this to his friend Paul Hanson, whose father, A. D. Hanson, was co-owner of the Hanson-Holden bookstore in Cedar Rapids. It happened that Paul had recently rented an office and set himself up as a commercial photographer.

"Why don't you come down there with me?" Paul suggested.

So in the spring of 1911 Grant moved into the office with Paul. PAUL C. HANSON, PHOTOGRAPHER, AND GRANT D. WOOD, ILLUSTRATOR, were lettered on the door. They wore smocks or long coats and had craftsmen's lamps. The office was filled with tripods, cameras, easels, drawing boards, paints and brushes. They didn't have any darkroom, however, and Paul had to take his films out like the rankest amateur for developing. Grant was ready to illustrate anything, but there was no demand for his services. The rent for the office was twenty dollars a month, and it began to pile up.

They thought of various devices to drum up business. On April 17, 1911, a postcard came through the mails to Henry S. Ely, a Cedar Rapids real-estate dealer. On one side was pictured his Knollwood Place home. On the back was written: "This is a small part of an 8 × 10 picture which is well composed. If interested address Hanson & Wood, Room 10 Jim Block, City."

Though later Ely was to become one of Grant's chief sponsors, at the time he hadn't heard of Hanson & Wood, and wasn't interested.

Paul was engaged to marry Vida Hatter, whom he had met while working as a draftsman in Dubuque, where she was a stenographer. He wrote her that business was a little slow and perhaps they had better postpone the wedding for a while. Vida had other ideas, and came to Cedar Rapids. They were married on May 29, 1911.

The attractive and vigorous Vida looked into her husband's business affairs and found them in a sorry state. She was humiliated by a dunning letter for the office rent. It spoke of legal action and of vacating the premises. Without telling Paul, she went to the landlord and told him that the rent would be paid if she had to pay it herself. She went downtown and got a job the same day. When she reached home that night and told him what she had done, Paul was furious. He didn't want his wife to work, and he felt that her visit to the landlord was a business embarrassment of the worst kind. The letter, he explained, was just a form; it didn't mean a thing. The landlord in fact was a schoolmate of his and a good friend.

Paul soon settled the matter by going out of business. He went back to work in his father's bookstore, and Grant went to Minneapolis for his second summer at the Handicraft Guild. But Batchelder meanwhile had established the Throop Polytechnic Institute, a combined art center and school at Pasadena, California, and didn't have time to spend summers in Minnesota. There was no further reason for study at the Handicraft Guild, so Grant's second summer there became his last.

FIVE

"A Little Discouraged"

THAT FALL, Grant took the Iowa teacher's examination, with indifferent results. He had been reading American history, in connection with some murals he hoped to paint, and he scored a brilliant 98 in the subject. He got 86 in writing, 81 in arithmetic and 80 in didactics. But he fell to the low 70s in reading, geography and spelling, to a miserable 49 in grammar and to a feeble 32 in vocational music. The grades weren't high enough to entitle him to a standard teacher's certificate. He was given a provisional certificate, good for one year.

He taught the 1911–12 term at Rosedale, a one-room country school three miles outside Cedar Rapids. As a teacher he didn't seem impressive—his manner was mild, his speech slow and his voice bland; he stammered and flushed easily; although his head was large, his eyes were small and he had already begun to develop the habit of squinting. He frequently overslept and reached the school late. He hated cold weather and persuaded one of the boys to come early to build the fire.

The cold dogged him everywhere that winter. He slept in a cold room and walked to and from the school. During part of the winter, he attended an art class three nights a week at the State University of Iowa, which entailed riding a cold and clattering interurban the twenty-eight miles from Cedar Rapids to Iowa City.

He simply walked into the university. No one greeted him and no one ever seemed to notice that he wasn't enrolled and didn't have the credits required for the course. He drew and painted with the rest of the students and showed his work to the professor, C. A.

Cumming, who nodded vaguely and wasn't impressed. Grant didn't like the instruction, and after three or four months stopped going. That was the "one year at the State University of Iowa" which he sometimes entered after his name. He used to call himself the only alumnus of S. U. I. who was never registered and who never paid any tuition. "That's the way a university should be run," he declared. "I didn't get an education, and I didn't owe them a cent. When you don't get anything, you shouldn't have to pay."

Grant's salary for teaching at Rosedale was thirty-five dollars a month, and the pupils fared well under him. There were twenty-one of them, ranging in age from six to thirteen. They learned more drawing than is usually the case at such a country school, and they took home highly satisfactory grades in other subjects. He was liberal with 95s: he never liked to discourage a student with a low grade. He did give Freddie Condon a 68 in spelling and a 60 in arithmetic at mid-term, but Freddie came back at the end of the year with a 78 in arithmetic and an 88 in spelling, then called orthography.

Grant never considered teaching at Rosedale a second year. The prospect of taking another teacher's examination was one he didn't care to contemplate. Moreover, he had other interests. He and Paul Hanson went into partnership again, this time to write magazine articles.

Weeks of reading and research went into an article that finally appeared in the *Craftsman* entitled "Peer Gynt's Cabin and Other Log Houses Associated with the History and Romance of Norway." It read as though written by an inveterate globe-trotter. For their labors, Grant and Paul received twenty-five dollars, and divided it equally. They moved their headquarters to Chicago for a time, and sold an article called "Cabin in the Woods" describing a house an artist had built outside of Chicago of sixty-four-foot timbers. This netted them another twenty-five dollars, and closed

37

their books in the magazine-writing business. They went back to
Cedar Rapids.

They learned to do a clog dance that sounded well enough on
top of a table, and talked of starting a brother act in a show. It
never got beyond the joking stage: Paul was tall and angular,
while Grant was short and round. Grant thought seriously of becoming a cartoonist. He had an idea that the way to get started as
a cartoonist was to popularize some phrase which, through mere
repetition, finally becomes funny. The idea has worked well
enough for others since, but the phrase Grant picked on was
"Mop that one up," and he repeated it over and over until Paul
and Vida were ready to brain him if they ever heard the wretched
expression again.

Grant worked again that fall in Kate Loomis' shop, and helped
her decorate her new home. His first oil to be signed "Grant
Wood" was painted for her. He had previously used the initials
"G.D.W." but dropped his middle name, DeVolson, in the belief
that the "D" spoiled the rhythm of his name. The painting was
an overmantel piece showing a low spot in a forest with jack-in-
the-pulpits growing among the tree roots and with rolling hills in
the background. Grant put it in an oak frame and made metal
sconces to go on either side—part of his shopwork.

His artistic ambitions were high at this time and he spent a
good part of the winter working on a set of murals that he hoped
to do in Washington High School. The murals were to deal with
the history of Iowa, and he spent feverish weeks in library research.
He worked over his designs in black and white until they satisfied
him; then he did them in opaque water colors to work out his color
scheme. From his earliest years he had been anxious to do some
public work that would cause people to take notice. He liked to
be known and, above all, he liked to be liked. A member of the
school board, probably without realizing that his words were caus-

ing Grant to work day and night, had encouraged him to believe that the murals would be accepted. This proved to be far from the case. Without even looking at the designs, the school board decided that nothing of the kind was wanted—or at least that no money was available for such a purpose. The sketches for the murals became worthless, and for the next few months Grant mourned over the corpse of this project.

In the spring of 1913, he got a job at sixteen dollars a week at the Kalo Silversmiths Shop in Chicago. The following October, he registered for night classes at the Art Institute of Chicago and attended for a little more than a month. He resumed study at the institute at the end of January, 1914, and attended fairly regularly for five months. Classes were held three nights a week, from 7:00 to 9:30 P. M.

At the Kalo shop, he kept aloof, barely speaking to most of his fellow workmen, but he did make one solid friend at the shop in Christopher Haga, a Norwegian immigrant and a skilled craftsman. Haga had saved some money and wanted to go into business for himself. He liked Grant's designs and, though Grant had no money to contribute, offered to take him into partnership. They gave up their jobs, rented a farmhouse in suburban Park Ridge, and set up a shop in a second-floor bedroom. They called their place the Wolund Shop, after the god of the silversmiths in a Norwegian saga. It was Grant who thought of the name; he had read the saga while researching for "Peer Gynt's Cabin." Two other Norwegian immigrant silversmiths, B. B. Anderson and Daniel Pedersen, later moved into the house with them, but kept their jobs at Kalo's. Each of the four paid four dollars a week for room and board. That was enough to pay the rent and keep the house in plenty of food—steaks, stews, pies, bacon and eggs. They took turns doing the cooking and housework. Haga and Grant slept late and worked late, and occasionally they were still at work when Anderson and Pedersen got up the next morning to go to Kalo's.

At Park Ridge the general opinion of Grant's ability was not high. Haga praised his designs, but Anderson and Pedersen thought them not exceptional. They didn't regard him as a first-class chaser. He seemed listless, slow and unsure of himself. Paul Hanson had told Vida to save everything she could of Grant's because some day he would be famous, but such a thought never occurred to the Norwegian craftsmen.

The Wolund Shop lasted for a year and a half, from June, 1914, to January, 1916. In good weather, Haga and Grant strung a net in the yard and played a kind of makeshift tennis with Anderson and Pedersen. During rainstorms, Grant sometimes amazed his friends by going naked into the yard for a shower bath; he claimed he got a better bath that way than he did from the round wooden tub in the house. Occasionally he went to dinner at some Norwegian friend's home, and on Saturday nights he usually put on his good suit, took the Northwestern train thirteen miles to downtown Chicago, and saw a movie. He had no friends among girls and seldom spoke of women. He didn't drink or smoke. He was twenty-four but he seemed hardly more than adolescent.

During the summer of 1915, he and Haga went "pearlfishing" in Iowa. They canoed thirty miles down the Cedar River gathering clams, from which they removed the slug pearls. Paul and Vida Hanson joined them at the end of the trip, and they decided on a month's vacation. They got up a party that included Ralph and Stella Conybeare, the latter a cousin of Grant's, and went to Ellis Park, where they stayed in cabins during August.

Grant and Haga were back at the Wolund Shop during the fall of 1915, to take advantage of what Christmas business there was. Some of the jewelry designs Grant made at that time found their way into scrapbooks at the Chicago Public Library. He made a silver repoussé jewel box, with a girl swimmer chased on the cover and with one of his pinkish slug pearls in her hand, which was exhibited at the Art Institute as a fine piece of workmanship and was later sold by the Wolund Shop.

At the end of 1915, Grant and Haga admitted what had been apparent for some time: they weren't making any money. With the war on in Europe, the cost of materials had gone up and the demand for hand-wrought jewelry had gone down. They went out of business.

Grant was as close to panic as he ever got. With only about twenty-five dollars to his name, he went to the Art Institute and arranged to attend classes both day and night. He took the school administrators back through the records and convinced them that, because of absences, he was entitled to two months of night classes free. Then on January 3, 1916, he registered for the first time as a full-fledged student, so he could attend day classes. He had to pay a five-dollar matriculation fee, and five dollars toward his day tuition. If he had ever entertained the thought that the Wolund Shop could take the place of an artistic career, he now gave it up. On his previous night-school cards he had described himself as a "metalworker"; now, on his registration card, he gave his occupation as "fresco painter."

He hoped that something would turn up to keep him going. He had in mind getting a part-time job, to pay at least for his board. It had been a mistake to go in for something that took up too much of his time. What he wanted was just enough work to enable him to eat while he attended the art school. During the first few days of his day-and-night study, he received the only comment ever recorded on his work at the Art Institute—an honorable mention in the life class of Antonin Sterba.

Nothing did turn up. At the end of a week, his money was gone. He borrowed just enough from a friend in Cedar Rapids to pay his train fare home, and on January 14, eleven days after he had matriculated, and despite the fact that he could have had six

41

more weeks of night classes free, he left Chicago and the Art Institute for good. He was nearly six years out of high school, and in that time had received what amounted to less than a full year's instruction.

"I was a little discouraged," he said. "It was the only time in my life that I couldn't find a job of some sort. On a wild chance I wrote to a friend in Cedar Rapids and he sent me a small check. I came back home again, a ragged failure—and my mother was glad to see me."

At Home in a Shack

PAUL and Vida Hanson didn't consider themselves hard up. They had a respectable bank account, and Paul's credit rating was high. Nevertheless they moved into the woods outside Cedar Rapids as an economy measure. Nearly a third of their income was going for rent, and they had worked out a plan to finance the building of a home of their own. Why live only for landlords?

So Paul bought some lots near Indian Creek in the subsequently absorbed subdivision of Kenwood and built a tarpaper-covered shack to live in while they were saving money. The shack had one room, eight by sixteen feet—pretty small, but Vida decided that if they had everything small to go with it, it would be big enough.

She grew blisters on her hands cutting and hacking their mattress in two, and Paul built Pullmanlike bunks in one side. They got a small stove that would do for both cooking and heating, and a small table. Their parents strongly objected to their living in this style, but they went ahead with their plan. During the cold months they rented an apartment in Cedar Rapids.

Paul and his friend Lon Dennis then built a second shack, to be used as a shop. It was a little bigger, ten by sixteen feet—the size being determined by the length of the boards they were able to get—but it wasn't covered with tarpaper. That second shack, or shop, was standing close to the Hansons' midget house when Grant came back from the Art Institute.

Grant found his mother about to be evicted from their home. After fifteen years, she had exhausted her financial resources. First she had used what Maryville left, then a thousand dollars from the sale of part of their lot, then what she had received from her father's estate, and lastly all she could borrow against the place. Now there was no money, no way of paying interest on the mortgage, and nothing to do but prepare to move.

The Commercial Trust and Savings Bank of Cedar Rapids had obtained a judgment against her for $5,222. On May 20, 1916, the old house was sold under the sheriff's hammer to the bank for the amount of indebtedness. As it happened, there was a place to which Grant and Mrs. Wood could go where they would be entirely welcome. It was the shack next to the Hansons in Kenwood. And that is where they went.

The Wood and Hanson shacks, which looked like overnight cabins at a tourist camp, were scarcely fifteen yards apart. They sat on top of a wooded hill beside Indian Creek. A footpath led up to them from a bridge a quarter of a mile downstream, and another path led to a spot where the creek could be crossed by stepping from stone to stone.

Mrs. Wood—"Woody," as Vida always called her—didn't grieve. She and Paul were firm in the belief that Grant had a great future, and she was glad to have him home. Inside the shop, with its row of windows intended to light a workbench, she sat quietly in her old rocking chair—a short-armed piece with its back straight up when at rest, which had been in her family for seven generations. She sewed and cooked.

When the weather was right, she pulled stockings over her arms to protect them from the hazel brush and went into the woods to look for food. Vida often went with her on these trips. They were interested not only in mushrooms and common greens such as dandelions but in anything else that looked "kinda tender." They had read in a magazine that mullen leaves were good to eat. The magazine was quite definite on the point, but they never were able to cook them enough to get the furry taste out. They tried cooking clams from Indian Creek and had still worse luck; the clams were the toughest morsels they had yet gotten into their kettles.

AT HOME IN A SHACK

After they had boiled for hours, Grant got out a meat grinder and ground them up; then Mrs. Wood and Vida made clam soup. They ate it, without much enthusiasm.

"It's awfully hard for me to say I like this stuff," Paul admitted.

Mrs. Wood found elderberries, blackberries and gooseberries in the woods. She picked cherries on half shares in neighboring groves, and canned and made jellies. Grant, the Hansons and the Conybeares often went swimming at Cook's Pond, a walk of two miles, and on the way back stopped at farms along the route to pick up corn, melons and garden vegetables for little or nothing. It cannot be said that Grant ever went hungry, except perhaps for a few days when he was away from home and out of money, but from a meat-eater's standpoint the fare at Kenwood was extremely simple. Mrs. Wood and Vida planned one big meal a day, and the big meal was the one at which everybody had all the fried potatoes he wanted.

At this low point in his life, Grant seemed more deliberate than ever. Indian Creek flows slowly between the hills of Kenwood; without moving much water, it is broad and deep and for the most part difficult to cross. Even the air seems to drift about slowly, pausing to pick up vegetable odors. It is no place to be in a hurry.

Grant Wood didn't hurry. He hardly looked for work, though he sometimes came upon it. He went on hiking trips up the creek, and sketched and painted. He went swimming, and sketched and painted. When it rained, he looked out of the window, and sketched and painted.

He did odd jobs about the shack. He made more glue flowers. He braided chair bottoms of cornhusks, which held up well, and tried the same thing with cattails, which didn't. He got a little work decorating people's homes. He was beginning to be a handy man, though not in the ordinary sense—he was called in only when an artistic touch was required.

45

As a pupil of Batchelder, he believed in combining utility and simplicity. One of his prejudices was against the common type of screen door. He wanted a screen door all in straight lines, one that wouldn't sag or give. He especially disliked fretwork across the corners. "That fretwork is all cross-grained," he would say. "It doesn't add anything to the strength of the door and it isn't decorative." On Paul's shop he put a masterful screen door, of inch-and-a-quarter framework, which still swung after years of battering.

He used his metalcraft, a discarded piece of copperplating, and the bottom of a broken milk bottle to make a hurricane lamp which he hung on the outside over the door. Mrs. Wood, or Paul or Vida or Nan, used to light the candle in the lamp if it got dark before Grant reached home: he liked to see it burning as he came up the path.

The shop rested on a slope with its back corners propped up, so that only the front part touched the ground. Grant cut a trap door in the floor so his mother could sweep dust through it. This idea backfired: drafts of wind blew the dust back into the house, and he finally had to nail the trap door shut. An improvised drain worked better. He cut a round hole in the floor next to the wash-stand and stuck an old talking-machine horn in it; the washbasin could be emptied into the mouth of the horn. Instead of putting in bunks, as the Hansons did, he made himself a low cot, which fitted under the small bed on which his mother slept. Grant's cot could be rolled out at night, and took up no space in the daytime. He built cabinets for his mother's canned goods and his tools, and laid a tile porch floor at the door.

There was no cellar or cave under the one-room shop so he built an outdoor cooler. It consisted of a four-foot ladder of shelves, like a narrow bookcase, with a pan of water fastened to the top shelf and a burlap cover draped over the entire contraption. The burlap, acting as a wick, drew water from the pan to keep itself moist. The moisture evaporated, taking heat with it and cooling whatever was on the shelves; butter kept solid on the hottest days. To get it away from ants, Grant suspended the cooler from a tree limb, like an Indian mummy. It could be raised and lowered by means of a rope and pulley.

Paul was making twelve dollars a week in his father's store and divided his check equally with Grant. Whenever Vida thought about it she really became indignant; a friend was a friend, she told Paul, but when it came to giving him half of your pay every week it was carrying things too far. Paul, however, kept on dividing his paycheck. Grant took the money without so much as a thank you; Paul knew he appreciated it and there wasn't anything to add to that.

Mrs. Wood had a few fixed ideas. One was that they should have their main meal at midday, though everyone else wanted it at night. She refused to get glasses, even after she had to give up reading and sewing at night, because she thought she would look "dreadful" in them. In the main, however, she let matters take their course. Whatever Grant thought they should do, they did.

Jack Wood had become an automobile mechanic and was living his own life. Frank, who had married Claire A. Peck in 1911, was trying to get an automobile accessory business well established in Waterloo, Iowa. Nan spent some of her time in the shack, and some with her maiden aunt, Sarah Wood.

Grant was painting chiefly flowers and landscapes. He did a quaking aspen tree for Nan on her seventeenth birthday. He spent a good deal of time teaching what he knew to Nan, and she later became a recognized artist. When Clarabelle Weaver asked him and some of his friends for a Sunday dinner, he used her paints to do a landscape for her during the afternoon. He was likely to present a painting to anyone who had done him a small favor.

He had been having trouble with faces and thought he had lost the ability to draw or paint them. When he included figures, he turned their heads away, left them without heads at all, or filled in expressionless features. A drawing he made of a group of boys around a swimming hole shows faces hardly better than those a child puts on a cat. He was twenty-five years old—for some reason he had begun giving his age as a year less than it was, a practice he continued for the rest of his life—but he had drawn faces better when he was fifteen.

He got over this trouble when he painted a portrait of Vida, which was to become his first portrait to be exhibited. Vida never liked it. Her profile was painted even and strong, but she thought her nose was too big, and she didn't like the way Grant emphasized it, or the way he had her do her hair up in back, for balance.

The Hansons first child, Robert, was born in Kenwood. Grant took a great interest in the baby and looked after it several evenings while Paul and Vida went out. He would stare at Vida when she was nursing it until she became ill at ease. Then one day he asked her to pose for a mother-and-child figure, which seemed to explain his unusual interest, and she agreed. For several days, at nursing hours, she sat at a window with her back partly turned and the light across her while he worked on a figure so small that he could cover it with his hand. He wouldn't let her see it, and when it was done he took it home with him. A week later he brought it back and placed it on the table. What he had done was a mother-and-child nude. Vida was embarrassed and angry. Yet she could see that it was a finely done thing.

She didn't destroy it intentionally. It was in plaster, covered with gilt bedstead paint, and was accidentally knocked to the floor and broken. Grant said it didn't make any difference. Vida thought he had decided it wasn't the right thing to do. Later, when Bobby Hanson was two years old, Grant made a relief of him which captured the child's soft lines and wistful expression, and this Vida kept.

48

She also kept Grant's portrait of her for several years, until after his name had become known. But she still didn't like it, so she offered it for sale. Yet she felt wretched when it was actually sold and wondered if there was any way of getting it back. There wasn't. Band leader Wayne King had bought it for $250.

SEVEN

The Builders

PAUL's plan to build a house was expanded. He and Grant decided to build two houses. Grant couldn't put up any money, but Paul could arrange the money and credit for the materials, and they planned to do all the work themselves. Grant agreed to buy one of the houses when they were finished.

They started work on the houses during the summer of 1916, at a place about a half mile from the shacks and on the other side of Indian Creek. Paul took time off from working in his father's store. Their carpentry experience consisted chiefly of their manual training in high school, and they frequently consulted Bradford's *Book of Carpentry* and *Book of Joinery*.

They were workmen cut from different molds. When it came to shingling a roof, Paul would cover half the space while Grant was tapping a dozen shingles into place. He mooned over this kind of work, thought of things to talk about, and of a hundred other things to do. When Paul was told that according to the records Grant had worked for a short time as a machinist's assistant, he could remember no such thing and found it difficult to believe: "It would have gone against every grain in his body." Vida agreed: "You never thought of Grant as working at all, because what he did was just what he wanted to do."

And it seemed to Paul that Grant didn't have any nerves. On one occasion Grant was sharpening a saw in a partly completed basement of one of the houses. He had the saw clamped in a vise so that the teeth of the saw stuck up four or five inches above the jaws of the vise. Every time he drew the file across it, the saw screeched and moaned like the agonies of the damned. Paul was at some distance, but could stand it no longer. He ran down the steps shouting, "Damn it, Grant, cut out that racket." Grant was bewildered. He stared blankly at Paul. "Has that been making a noise that bothered you?" The work on the saw was the kind that didn't require his attention, and he hadn't noticed anything.

When it came to close fittings, cabinetmaking or anything intricate, however, Grant was ahead of Paul. Grant had drawn the plans for the houses and had insisted on hip roofs—four-planed affairs coming to a point in the center. Paul didn't know how to make a hip roof and very much wanted plain gable roofs. Grant said he would solve all the problems. He consulted texts at the library, squeezed what he could from Bradford's books, and made his drawings. He still wasn't sure that he knew exactly how to proceed, so he decided to test his knowledge. There was an outhouse a short distance down the slope from the Wood and Hanson shacks. It was always referred to as "The Greenhouse." To gain experience, Grant put a hip roof on the outhouse, and this became the model for the roofs on the houses.

Carpenters in the neighborhood were betting that Grant and Paul would never get the houses up—at least not with hip roofs on them. One day while they were at work, a carpenter and his ten-year-old son stopped in the street. The son leaned out of the car window and asked: "Did you buy that lumber straight or did you get it ready-cut?" When Grant and Paul assured him they had bought it straight, the boy, pleased, said: "See, Dad, I told you so," then volunteered: "Dad said you fellows wouldn't know enough to cut lumber for a hip roof."

The houses didn't take shape very rapidly. No one seemed to be in a hurry to get them up, or to be concerned about the fact that they were living in close quarters and on plain food. On one occasion, Grant, Paul and Vida, discussing their life in Kenwood, agreed there was only one thing wrong: they didn't have enough social life. It was like Thirissa Wood's opinion of pioneer Ohio: "All that appears to be wanting is society."

Vida's sister, Dawn Hatter, visited her while they were living in the shacks. It was no trouble for the Hansons, or the Woods either, to keep guests in good weather; they took camp chairs, pillows and blankets and slept outdoors. The guests ate potatoes. Grant accompanied Dawn on excursions up the creek. He and the Hansons gave a barn dance for her in a nearby dairy barn, using borrowed phonograph records. The four went frequently to Cook's Pond to swim.

Grant and Paul passed for good swimmers, in a landlocked country. The pond, a spring-fed lake with a single outlet running down a ravine, covered several acres. They could swim out to an island and then to another shore—a distance of perhaps four hundred yards. Paul and Vida used to cite this ability in Grant's defense when people with a low opinion of art sometimes spoke of him as lazy or effeminate.

One day Grant fished a huge iron kettle from the pond and had Paul—who hadn't been discouraged by the failure of the Hanson & Wood Studio and still carried a camera—take a picture of him as he turned it upside down on his head. With the feet of the kettle sticking up and the slime from it running down over his body, he looked like a prehistoric monster in the picture. It gave him an idea.

A hoax had recently appeared in one of the Cedar Rapids papers. A reporter claimed to have discovered a kitchen, utensils, and human bones in Horsethief's Cave, northeast of Kenwood. For proof, the paper offered a picture of Horsethief's Chimney, a pipe sticking out of the ground, supposedly connected with a cookstove in a deep recess of the cave. Actually, as Grant and Paul knew, the pipe was an old well casing from which the ground had washed away, and though the cave may have harbored a few horsethieves it had no deep recesses. They had some hearty laughs, watching from a nearby hillside, as a crowd gathered at the mouth of the cave the Sunday the story appeared. Some of the curious crawled through the cave's narrow entrance in their Sunday clothes and came out wet and muddy.

Grant's idea was to sell the papers a superhoax. He carved a foot eighteen inches long out of wood and made footprints in the ravine leading from Cook's Pond. With his monster picture and the footprints as proof, he tried to convince the newspapers that a giant had risen up from the pond and then clumped off down the ravine. As it turned out, he didn't succeed in interesting the papers in his story. But he did use the footprints: he cast them in concrete and laid them as a sidewalk from front to back of the house he was to occupy; the concrete footprints were spaced so that it looked as though a giant had just knocked at the front door and then hurried around the corner of the house.

Paul, Vida and Grant became well acquainted with the farmers between Cook's Pond and the Kenwood woods. When they stopped to buy food, it was hard to keep the farm wives from giving them more than they could carry. Paul bought a heifer at one of the farms, and Grant went with him to get it. The beast didn't know what was in store for her, but she didn't think she'd like it, and before they were halfway back she refused to go farther. Grant and Paul dragged her by the halter on her knees for a while, then gave up, tied her to a fence post, and went home. Both were exhausted and out of humor from the struggle, and Grant decided there was no sense to buying a heifer anyhow.

"Why pay fifteen dollars for a heifer when you can get a calf for three dollars and raise it?" he demanded.

Paul reminded him that you would have to feed milk to a calf, and that buying milk for such a purpose was out of the question.

"I wouldn't give it any milk," Grant declared, and insisted on the point until Paul and Vida started laughing and good humor was restored.

But humor and seriousness were mixed in Grant. He remembered the incident, later bought a calf that had hardly found its legs, and didn't give it any milk. He fed it an oatmeal gruel, and it did all that can be expected of a calf: it grew into a cow, and pastured on the Kenwood meadows.

Dawn came for more visits, and Grant's interest in her seemed to grow. Like Vida, she was handsome and lively—an interested and human sort of a girl, whose face lit up quickly at a suggestion of humor or common understanding. Grant said he wanted to marry her, but he lacked the reckless passion or other incentives necessary to conclude such matters. At the rate he was going the courtship might have lasted ten years.

"I'd like to marry Dawn, but I have my mother and sister," he told Vida.

Dawn settled the matter by marrying someone else.

The two houses were not ready by the fall of 1916. Indian summer came and went, and Grant and Paul kicked through fallen leaves as they came up the hill. Then the Hansons moved into town for the cold months. Nan went to stay with her aunt. Mrs. Wood and Grant moved from the shop to the Hanson tarpaper-covered shack, which was warmer.

It was one of the coldest winters on record. The temperature went from zero to twenty below and then alternated back and forth between the two. Mrs. Wood and Grant spent several days under comforts in the bunks to keep warm; even a red-hot stove wouldn't heat the place. However, they were never out of groceries, and when people sometimes left baskets of food at the door, they resented it. Paul still divided his pay, and they had enough potatoes and bread. Grant set some traps in the snow and caught a few rabbits. He preferred potatoes, however; he hated rabbit meat.

They had a feast on Christmas—a duck dinner, they called it.

Mrs. Wood bought a piece of round steak. Grant had her wrap it around a stick and cover it with muslin. Then he carved the end of the stick into a duck's head. In later years, when his manner of living had greatly improved, he often remembered that meal.

"I put a lot of style and design into that duck's head," he said.

Artist in Uniform

GRANT and Paul finished the two houses in the spring of 1917 and the Woods moved from the shack to their new home. Their house was a small, two-level affair: you entered a second-floor living room from the ground level at the front and walked downstairs to a semibasement kitchen and dining room. An iron stove enclosed in brick, off the kitchen, served as a furnace and there were two upstairs bedrooms. Grant did his painting in the dining room, which looked out on a sloping back yard.

His artistic ideas at this time, and for years afterward, were based on popular conceptions of what an artist should be like, and he spent a lot of time waiting for inspiration. He thought he should be seized by an overwhelming desire to paint, that he would then be able to paint with rapid strokes, and that he would be stirred by the result.

That kind of inspiration never came. His ideas, even trivial ones, took shape gradually, and he was one of the slowest painters ever to take up a brush. Sometimes he would paint a landscape in the course of an afternoon, but before he considered it finished he would stand before it for hours, his feet apart, swaying back and forth, occasionally dabbing here and there.

Housewives with decorating problems didn't understand this. Grant kept pictures for weeks and months—pictures they had seen and that seemed perfectly complete—while they stared at blank places on their walls. When they inquired, Grant told them he still had some touching up to do. Sometimes they never got delivery, and what became of the paintings no one knew.

His income from painting was a standing joke among his

friends. His potboilers—flowers and landscapes—usually brought five or ten dollars. One year it was suggested to him that he file an income-tax report, just to make sure that everything was all right. He went to the internal revenue office and gave what figures he could remember.

After looking at the figures, the collector good-naturedly told him he didn't need to make a report. "You may consider," said the collector, "that your income from painting is offset by the cost of frames."

His friends tried to persuade him to charge more for decorating. Cedar Rapids is notable for the production of breakfast foods, both the National Oats and the Quaker Oats companies being located there. "Charge as though you were working at Quaker Oats," Paul Hanson and Ralph Conybeare used to tell him. "You ought to get as much as those fellows over there. Charge 'em for the time you spend making designs." Grant listened to the advice but didn't follow it. If he worked for somebody he knew, he didn't like to charge anything, and he gave away, or threw away, as many paintings as he sold. He was usually glad to get rid of anything he had finished. People said he was never satisfied with a picture until at last he had completed it; then he didn't care for it at all.

He lined the kitchen with cabinets and built racks, shelves and drawers in one of the two upstairs bedrooms for his paints, canvases, pressboard panels, and his metal- and woodworking tools. He seemed almost too orderly for an artist and never collected trash or personal articles. The only permanent decorative pieces in his room were a water color on cream paper of a sprig of fat currants, which he had painted eleven years before when he was fifteen, and a small statuette of Athena reaching for her sandal. He was painting wistful scenes such as *The Dutchman's, Feeding the Chickens*, and *The Horse Trader's*.

Despite his indifferent attitude toward money, the Woods' fortunes picked up in 1917. The house had been bought from Paul on a contract, and there was nothing urgent about the payments. Grant's frames didn't cost as much as the revenue collector imagined, because he made them all himself. He got more decorating work than formerly and though prices of food were going up because of the war, Mrs. Wood began setting a better table.

Part of his work was for Henry S. Ely. The realtor had begun building small, material-saving houses when the war put a stop to ordinary construction. Grant made doll-sized models of the houses and put them in artistic surroundings. He lacquered ordinary sponges and set them among the houses for trees. They looked a good deal like the globular trees that later made their appearance in his paintings. He dipped newspapers in glue, molded them into shrubbery shapes, and painted them green. He used revolving chandelier prisms and mica balls to get night lighting effects. He thatched roofs for the models with straw and twine. He put stiffening in a handkerchief, shaped it into a model of the Liberty Bell, including the crack, and painted it with dull radiator gold. He got realistic touches in his settings by including ash heaps, paper hollyhocks, half-mowed lawns and forgotten lawn mowers, children's toys and figures in working clothes. Some of his settings could be folded into a box and then opened again with the houses in place. One was a jack-in-the-box which flew open when a string was pulled. He also drew pamphlet and program covers, and lettered advertisements. The letters were good, and they moved with dignity through such doggerel as "Every Bird and Bee that Lights, Finds a Home in Vernon Heights." Ely was well satisfied with Grant's work.

Since his mother and sister were dependent on him, he had been placed in Class 3C in the draft and was passed over in the first draft call in September. Later, other family arrangements were made for the very little money Mrs. Wood needed to keep house, and Grant enlisted as a private in the army. He was sent to Camp

Dodge, outside Des Moines, where he spent a good part of his training period making pencil portraits of his comrades and officers. He charged privates twenty-five cents and officers one dollar for the portraits—at least these were his prices when anyone offered to pay him. He didn't ask for payment, and the officer didn't think to offer it, when he made a portrait of his company commander, Captain George E. Proud.

Captain Proud was getting ready to go into town when a sergeant came in to say there was a man outside who wanted to make a sketch of him. The captain was in a hurry, but told the sergeant to bring him in. It didn't take Grant more than ten or fifteen minutes to make the sketch. Proud scarcely looked at it at the time, and afterward didn't remember Grant's name; he only remembered that Grant had said he was a mural painter. When he was back practicing law at Arapahoe, Nebraska, however, Proud found the sketch among his things, liked it and had it framed. It hung on his office wall for fifteen years before someone happened to notice it was a Grant Wood portrait.

Grant's stay at Camp Dodge promised to be pleasant. He was excused from the more onerous military duties, given a sidecar motorcycle, and told to go about making historic records. Then he contracted anthrax, and nearly died. When he recovered, he was sent to Washington to do camouflage work. He served as a private in Company B, Regiment 97, United States Engineers, and was in charge of the paint tent. He made clay models of field-gun positions and helped camouflage artillery pieces. Before-and-after photographs of a cannon he helped camouflage were on display for several years at the Smithsonian Institution.

He was still in Washington when the war ended, and was transferred back to Camp Dodge. He arrived home on Christmas Eve, 1918. The Woods gathered to welcome him, and the family experiences were gone over. Grant said little about the army; his military experience appeared to have made slight impression on him.

59

He had to go back to Camp Dodge for a brief stay before getting his discharge. Then he took up his painting where he left off.

The paintings included *The Old Sexton's Place,* a view of an old barn, and *Looking for Wigglers,* a boy gazing down a rain barrel. Times were good in Cedar Rapids in 1919, but again his paintings brought little money. When fall came, he was still wearing his army clothes. Two of his cousins on his mother's side were Charles and George Keeler. Charles Keeler was a metalworker, and George had done some etching, including a very good etching of the Old Capitol Building which is now university headquarters at Iowa City. The cousins exchanged artistic experiences with him, and George, in Grant's behalf, telephoned Miss Frances Prescott, principal of Jackson Junior High School.

"Would you consider hiring Grant Wood as an art teacher?" he asked.

Miss Prescott, tall, Irish, energetic and independent, replied with her usual vigor.

"What have I ever done to you that you want me to take Grant Wood as a teacher?" she demanded.

"Well, he was in the army, and he needs a job."

"Why, he might go off with the children and get lost somewhere. He may be a Pied Piper for all I know."

After these and similar protests, Miss Prescott agreed to take Grant if he could get a certificate. She once took a janitor who had been dismissed from four other schools and not only kept him but came to number him among her best friends. The matter of the certificate was delicate, but Grant avoided the standard examination by getting a Special Subject Certificate to teach art. He was employed as a part-time instructor, and appeared in an army coat and campaign hat for his first day of city teaching.

Miss Prescott was inclined to think she had made a mistake.

She looked at him severely, and wasn't encouraged by what she saw. He was wearing heavy, horn-rimmed glasses that sank into his face, and his large forehead and cleft chin jutted. He had a thyroid condition for which he had been given medical treatment in the army, and it tended to slow his already slow speech. He was self-conscious, he stammered, he even hiccoughed. He was twenty-eight years old but he couldn't look Miss Prescott in the eye, and glanced uneasily at everything else in the room. His habit of swaying from side to side never left him, and he varied it a little by teetering and weaving. Miss Prescott tried hard to think of a better way of expressing it, but there wasn't any: he just "looked dumb."

She outlined his duties and then concluded: "Now remember, I won't come near you for a month, but you've got to produce. You know what you were hired for, don't you?"

Grant didn't say anything. Miss Prescott showed him his classroom and hoped for the best. Even against all better judgment, she thought he was entitled to a fair trial. She didn't object when she found that one of his classes had spent the hour talking about how to catch rabbits with a ferret. Grant told her he couldn't use a class outline, as was then required, so she told him to throw it away.

At the end of the first semester, Grant came to her for help.

"Something came in my box today about grades," he began.

"Well, where's your class book?"

Grant handed her the class book. Miss Prescott looked inside. It contained nothing but the names of the students, followed by blank squares.

"Don't you know what kind of work they've been doing?"

"Certainly."

"All right, if I say John Jones, can't you tell me what kind of a grade he ought to have?"

"I don't know them by their names."

61

Miss Prescott thought it over. She attended his next class, and together they went around the room, stopping beside the pupils in the order they were listed. Grant decided upon the grades. Miss Prescott put them down.

NINE

The Imagination Isles

WHEN Miss Prescott moved from Jackson Junior High to the newly built McKinley High School, she understood she could take along anything that concerned the ninth grade or above. Ninth-grade children, she thought, were of an age to appreciate Italian art, so she took some prints of Italian paintings that she liked for her new hall.

Complaints reached the school board about the "theft" of these prints. The superintendent several times suggested to Miss Prescott that she return them. The complaints kept coming in. The superintendent jogged Miss Prescott about the matter until she became a little nettled.

"Why don't you *order* me to return them?"

It was more of a challenge than a suggestion, but the superintendent felt himself in a tight spot, so he issued a formal order for the return of the prints to Jackson. That closed the subject until one day the superintendent visited Miss Prescott at McKinley. As they walked down the hall, he paused in front of the Italian prints.

"Aren't these the pictures I told you to return to Jackson?"

"Yes, they are."

"You didn't return them?"

"No."

"I *ordered* you to, didn't I?"

"Yes, you did. Your skirts are entirely clean in this matter."

The prints are still hanging in McKinley High School. It wasn't often that Miss Prescott gave up something she liked.

And she liked Grant Wood. She liked him as a person and for

the things he did for the school, the program and annual covers he designed, the decorating he directed, the mural and model projects he started. One of his pupils won a hundred-dollar prize in a Victory Loan poster contest. So Grant had a secure berth at Jackson and, after the move in 1922, at McKinley. When he didn't arrive for his classes, Miss Prescott went and got him in her car. When people complained that the discipline in his classes was bad, that a babble of voices often could be heard outside his door, she reminded them that artists were not like everybody else. When she found that Grant was eating his lunch alone in his classroom, she edged him down the hall and pushed him through the door to the teachers' dining room.

"Here, boil this man an egg," she called, and slammed the door.

She also pushed him into public speaking, though it seemed the farthest thing possible from his abilities. She heard that he had refused to speak before a business club.

"I've just called them up and told them that you've changed your mind," she advised Grant. "You can talk about war art."

Grant was alarmed.

"You know I can't make a speech," he said.

"Get your easel out there. Put some war posters on it. Then tell them how it's done. That's all they want."

Grant made the speech. The posters kept falling off the easel, and he was considerably confused, but he got better attention than he expected. His slow delivery imposed a duty on his listeners, which most of them accepted—the duty of putting the sentences together. By the time the tag end of one sentence had been properly placed, another was started, and the listener had no chance to divert his attention.

For his first year of teaching at Jackson, Grant was paid nine hundred dollars. He taught in his private's uniform until he could buy clothes, and then began saving money. The Woods had been

SUSAN ANGEVINE SHAFFER · ANNO DOMINI MCMXXX

Courtesy of Van Vechten Shaffer

PORTRAIT OF SUSAN ANGEVINE SHAFFER

living on so little that it seemed a good income, and he kept on painting and making a little money on the side. By the spring of 1920, he was ready for a trip to Europe.

It was ten years since he and Marvin had graduated from high school. Back in those days when they were scraping glued paper off pictures for the exhibits, they had talked about going to Paris. Now they laid plans for a summer in what without question they had always regarded as the artistic center of the world. Although they couldn't leave until June, they had their passports by April, and had carefully calculated what they would spend. They didn't have much money, so they agreed to travel in day coaches, to get the cheapest possible quarters, and to drink nothing stronger than red wine. They knew no one in Paris; they simply went there as summer tourists to see what it was like and to do some painting.

During their stay in France the two young Iowans attracted public attention only once; that was on the Fourth of July, when Grant made a hot-air balloon, of sticks and tissue paper, which sailed in flames over the countryside with a crowd chasing after it. They stood at the foot of Paris monuments, tramped the surrounding country to paint in good weather, and visited museums when it rained. Grant was beginning to put on weight and to acquire the cherubic look of his later years. He was five feet seven inches tall and weighed 165 pounds. Marvin was thin and angular. In their Left Bank studio-room they did portraits of each other that exaggerated the difference—Marvin's face long and cadaverous, Grant's perfectly round. Grant labeled the portraits "Malnutrition" and "Overstimulation."

He wrote his letters home on picture postcards, scrawling in a large hand over the backs of several of them and then enclosing them in an envelope. He told of finishing a bas-relief of Marvin and of having it cast in bronze. He described with enthusiasm a visit they had made to Julien's Academy for Artists, and said he was crazy about the prospect of attending there—later. Along with these high artistic ambitions he had one other thing persistently on his mind: he kept urging his mother and Nan to put up plenty of green tomato pickles.

Marvin spent a good part of his summer waiting for Grant, who was as slow at getting himself ready to go out as he was at everything else. "We lose an hour a day while you're shaving," Marvin complained. Grant decided to let his beard grow. The beard came out pink, and the cleft in his chin divided it in two directions; his face was described as looking like an opened peanut-butter sandwich. Nor did this spectacular growth benefit Marvin: the hour that formerly had gone into shaving, Grant now spent in grooming his beard.

His paintings that summer included *Misty Day—Paris,* a view of the Carpeaux Fountain in the Luxembourg Gardens; *Square in Chatenay; Fountain of Voltaire; Tuileries Gate and the Obelisk; Round House, Paris;* and *Gardens, Versailles.* They were attempts to find in monuments and shaded walks the higher artistic level he associated with Europe, and his ambitions in this direction were still strong at the summer's end. When he and Marvin sailed for home, Grant was planning to return to Paris for a longer stay as soon as he could save enough money.

Back in Cedar Rapids, people were prepared to treat them with a new respect because they had been to Paris, but this proved almost impossible in Grant's case: he was still wearing the two-way beard when he stepped from the train, and it could be regarded only as funny. He called it a "Duncan hanging" and didn't shave it off until his pupils started a collection to buy him a razor. He began his second year at Jackson as a full-time instructor with a salary of twelve hundred dollars—the following year it was increased to fourteen hundred and in the fourth year to seventeen hundred.

His new acquaintance with French culture didn't affect his everyday tastes. He was likely to be seen examining junk piles for materials he could use, and he asked workmen at a machine shop to put aside leftover pieces of metal for him. Gadgets still interested him, and he invented an art compass that consisted of a board of colors and an arrow with flanges that would indicate the complementary colors. When pupils stole cigarettes from his coat in the cloakroom, he fashioned a trap, something like a mousetrap, which he kept in his pocket. For Miss Prescott's outer office he made a "Mourner's Bench" and carved ecclesiastical heads from wood to mount on its back.

Some of his activities were known in Cedar Rapids under the general heading of "Grant Wood's brainstorms." He began making what he at first called "Junk Flowers" and later "Lilies of the Alley." They looked like flowers but like no flowers that ever grew. From pots filled with plaster, painted bottle caps shot up to represent daisies. Tin leaves and petals were distributed among tendrils of wire and steel parings. Corks and clothespins became the centers of flowers, and springs, pins and odd pieces of junk found their places in the compositions. Grant continued making them for years, arranging and painting them carefully and then giving them away.

When his friend Charles Clark was trying unsuccessfully to rent his house, Grant suggested that he advertise a house "with a goldfish in every room." Clark got enough ten-cent-store goldfish to justify the advertisement, and it rented the house. That weird idea came about in this way: Nan had a goldfish that would eat from her hand; Grant spent a good deal of time watching it; the problem of renting a house came up; he put the two things together. On a short vacation trip to Cheley Camp in Colorado, he gathered a pile of bent and gnarled branches and, without cutting or bending, put them together in a human shape—"The Old

Man of the Mountain." It was just a matter of studying each branch until he found its proper place in the figure.

For Ely, he painted the "world's only outdoor mural." His original sketch in color was eleven by three inches and he enlarged it to eleven by three feet, showing a farmer, workmen and businessman grouped around an idealized woman holding aloft a model house—Paul Hanson posed as the carpenter in the picture. The outdoor mural, titled *Adoration of the Home,* stood for years under a canopy and lights in front of Ely & Co., Realtors, at a downtown intersection.

Grant's teaching methods were haphazard but effective. His focusing powers were highly developed: when he found a pupil with talent he was likely to hover over him for most of the class period, and a project was needed to keep the rest of the class at least partly engaged. One such project was the painting of 150 feet of frieze to decorate the high-school cafeteria. He had forty-five ninth-grade boys, and each boy was assigned to three or four feet of it. When the frieze band was completed, Grant mounted it between two revolving nail kegs, so it could be unrolled before an audience; then he wrote a descriptive address to be spoken when it was shown. If the Ely painting was the world's only outdoor mural, this was the world's only moving frieze.

"I invite you to come with me on a ten-minute trip through the Imagination Isles," the address began. "You shall see brilliantly colored trees of shape unknown to science, silhouetted against purple mountains, mountains whose snow-capped peaks pierce saffron skies. A sea, bluer even than the blue Mediterranean, beats against the base of each jewel-like island and frets itself into a snowy foam. Upon the sea float ships of romantic shape.

"No human body can visit these islands. Only the spirit can come. There is always room for all of us at any time. We may dip into the fragrant coolness of the indigo ocean. We may live as

68

long as we please in our choice of mother-of-pearl palaces without fear of intruding on anyone or of anyone intruding upon us. We pay no rent. We are guests.

"Our hosts on this trip are forty-five ninth-grade boys. They have produced the Imagination Isles in the art room of this school, using only the highest grade of oil paint and the very best imagination that is possible to be found locally.

"It is difficult to find people who can produce the material of dreams. A very very few people have this ability so strongly marked in youth that they are set apart and given special training. These people become musicians, poets and painters. They are valuable because they can lead others on in short vacation trips into the delightful land where their spirits are trained to dwell.

"Almost all of us have some dream-power in our childhood, but without encouragement it leaves us and we become bored and tired and ordinary. In most of our studies we deal only with material things. We become so busy about getting ourselves all nicely placed that we are apt to forget the dream spirit that is born in all of us.

"Then someday when we are physically comfortable we remember dimly a distant land we used to visit in our youth. We try to go again but we cannot. Our imagination machinery is withered. We become bored and cynical and hard spirited."

After several more paragraphs, the unrolling of the frieze proceeded. Grant took a lot of pride in the efforts of his students, even when, as sometimes happened, he retouched their work until they were unable to recognize it. Another of his projects was a model city, for which each student built a house, city hall, waterworks, factory or the like. These flimsy models, made by thirteen- and fourteen-year-olds, were serious matters to him. Miss Emma Grattan, the city art superintendent, brought to the school a man by the name of Hornbostle from Memphis who also had some ideas about model cities. Hornbostle outlined his ideas on the blackboard, and in the course of doing so was somewhat critical of the local models. The visitor had not gone far before Grant's face turned white. He rose from his chair, walked past the model-city expert to the cloakroom, put on his muffler and overcoat, and walked to the door. He bowed.

"Good afternoon," he said, and left for the day.

Sojourn in Paris

GRANT liked the drawings of children and primitive peoples because he considered them natural and honest, a means of expressing individual feeling without regard to the opinions of others. He thought it almost unfortunate that children in the seventh or eighth grade began to want their drawings to mean something to other people. Yet he realized that this desire to impress was what made his pupils interested in learning better methods. So he taught methods, told them that feeling and imagination were more important, and tried to keep up their interest.

Sometimes he gave prizes for good work in his classes. Paul Cummins, later of Fort Wayne, Indiana, got one of Grant's own paintings as a prize in an art poster contest. It was a small painting of a farmer with a team of horses. Cummins lived to refuse several hundred dollars for it; but at the time, he wasn't very glad to get it: he felt like a sissy, and his friends smirked at him as he walked back to his chair.

The tendency of those around him to look on art as effeminate was annoying to Grant. It had been a thorn in his side since early youth, and he spoke with some bitterness of "people who put painting on a level with tatting." He tried to cultivate more robust notions among his pupils by offering drawing subjects different from those conventionally used. A box of strawberries or a vase of flowers might be considered "sissy stuff," he pointed out, but nearly all students were interested in some form of transportation—airplanes, automobiles, wagons, or trains—and perspective could be taught as well with a model airplane, for instance, as with anything else.

Good-humored breaches of discipline as a rule didn't bother

71

him. When someone poured glue on one of the seats and a pupil
stuck fast to the chair, he was unable to suppress a smile, though
the prank ruined a suit of clothes. The parents came to the school,
demanding punishment of the guilty pupil, but Grant sent them
to Miss Prescott and refused to have anything to do with the
matter. Occasionally, however, the bedlam in his classes rose to a
pitch of distraction, and he was forced to call angrily for order.
When one of his bigger boys repeatedly talked back to him and
made smart remarks, Grant considered and discussed the possibility of landing a haymaker on the youth's jaw. One day as a
compromise he seized the youth by the shoulders and set him
down hard enough to test his spine.

He was serious about his teaching to the point of sometimes rating it more important than his painting—during low periods,
when his painting wasn't going well. However, he never actually
lost sight of the possibility that he would one day paint really important pictures. "If I ever become famous," he frequently said,
"there'll be only two people who aren't surprised: my mother and
Fan Prescott." He could have included Paul Hanson and some
others in that statement.

While he was trying to influence his pupils, teaching influenced
him. He got over his inability to look strangers in the eye, but
developed some of the mincing manners of an instructor of English, 3B. "How do you do, Mrs. Jones," he would say, with a rising
and falling inflection and an overpolite bow which had the effect
of putting acquaintances on their guard and keeping them at a
distance. When he returned from his first trip to Europe, he had
a cold, and his voice was husky. Paul and Vida told him that was
the voice he should cultivate. He actually did develop a lower
tone of voice, though it remained bland—"like the fragrance of
violets made audible." All his painting was in the mellow vein
of The Cowpath, and Grandma's Place.

He bought his first automobile in 1922. It was a dismal, secondhand affair. People used to ask him when he expected to get delivery on the rest of the car. Miss Prescott still had to go after him occasionally, because on cold mornings he couldn't get it started. His one great pride in the car was a homemade gadget he put on it to signal a left turn. When a lever was pushed to release it, a pointing hand flew out a foot or so, with its index finger on the turn. Grant called around the town, taking people he knew for rides and making left turns to demonstrate the hand. He had difficulty keeping the car between the curbs, when he was thinking of something else, and it didn't last long. When it gave out, he went back to telephoning different car owners, at appropriate intervals, to take him on painting and sketching tours, or in search of models and materials. His friends were the people who drove the cars on such trips.

There were times when people thought he might marry, but there were no sound reasons for these expectations. He took girls to parties and on picnics, but seemed uneasy at the prospect of being left alone with them and too deliberate for the pace of events. Besides he was still planning to study abroad.

"Do you think you'll ever marry?" Miss Prescott once asked him.

"I don't think so; not while my mother is living," he told her.

Despite his low earnings, he saved some money. His mother was a frugal housekeeper, and they made no pretenses. By the spring of 1923, he felt able to realize his desire to study at Julien's Academy in Paris. He applied for and was granted a year's leave of absence from teaching.

He was curiously young, for thirty-two. Most of his school friends had half-grown children and had settled into one groove or another. But Grant seemed to feel that he had not yet made a good start at anything, and that he had plenty of time. He was in Cedar Rapids most of the summer of 1923, then left for Paris.

He spent fourteen months in Europe, mostly in France, without learning a line of French or any other foreign language. He used to say it was an advantage not to know the language: "People took a protective interest in me." When he ate in restaurants where English wasn't spoken, he pointed to something on the menu and said *"Donnez-moi."* He learned the meaning of a few other words, but that was the only French expression he himself ever used.

Julien's was what was called purely a painting school—i.e., no formal lectures and no studying from books. It occupied a rambling old structure on the Rue du Dragon on the Left Bank. Each class had a leader who arranged for models and settled disputes. The students placed their easels in a semicircle around the model and drew or painted as they liked. The masters came in two or three times a week to criticize what was done. Under this system students normally learned as much from each other as from the masters, but since most of the students were French and Grant didn't speak their language, he was more or less ignored. His classmates referred to him indifferently as *"Tête de Bois"* (Woodenhead)—his first nickname.

Grant didn't mind the nickname, but he hated to be treated in such a casual way. No "protective interest" was being taken in him here. He decided to do something that would startle the class. The model was a male nude; he took a rear view and splashed his painting with dabs of red paint, so that it looked like a man with a bad case of measles. The picture had the effect he wanted: the students pronounced it terrible, and mustered their English or got translators to explain that the good name of the academy would be marred by such painting. They even took him to lunch and dinner to continue the lectures. Thereafter at least he didn't feel ignored.

The painting, *Spotted Man*, was somewhat improved in its finished state, much of the red having been painted under, but it was still nothing to interest a buyer. Perversely, Grant seemed to like it and to grow more fond of it as time passed. Too ungainly to be put away, too ugly to be sold, it stood for years in a corner of his studio. It was the first of his works in fifteen years—since the water color *Currants*—that he decided to keep for himself.

As it had been at the Art Institute, his attendance at Julien's became very irregular. A garret studio could be rented in Paris almost as cheaply as a room, and Grant had studio living quarters off the Boulevard Raspail. When he hadn't appeared at the academy for three weeks, an English fellow student called at his studio to see what was the matter. Despondent, haggard and moody, Grant greeted the Englishman coolly, and wanted to know whose business it was if he didn't choose to go to classes. The Englishman had the tact and the interest to deal with such a situation. Grant had talked to no one for days, and was soon telling more than he had ever told anyone before.

He said he didn't think he'd ever be an artist, that he didn't really have an education, that all his schooling had been broken into, that he didn't have much money and nothing to fall back on, and besides it was too late now to make it all up. He even told his personality troubles, his lack of self-confidence, his fevers of mortification, his seeming inability to meet people on an equal footing.

The Englishman listened and left. The next day he came back with an armload of books—Shakespeare, Dickens, Goethe's *Wilhelm Meister* and others. He told Grant that his trouble was an inferiority complex and that these books would cure it. He didn't merely drop the books and go, but stayed on, induced Grant to read aloud to him, and came back for more reading on succeeding days. Grant later said that, more than to any other man, he owed whatever poise he had developed to this Englishman, whose name he couldn't remember.

Grant went back to Julien's and so completely recovered from

75

his morbid depression that he dressed as a fish-in-a-net to attend the Quat-z-Arts ball (known to Americans as "The Cat's Ball"). He got gloriously cockeyed, as he described it, for this occasion, and though he had no ticket and was intending to crash the gate, considered it perfectly natural when he was met with a deep bow at the ballroom door. His host with much courtesy escorted him down a long hallway and opened a door. Grant stepped through it and found himself back on the street. He was by no means the first or the last guest received in this fashion; it was commonly said by Americans that you couldn't get into the ball if you had clothes on.

He didn't last out the winter in Paris. His old hatred of the cold returned, and he complained that he was comfortable only in bed. With several other American and French art students, he went to Sorrento on the Bay of Naples and stayed at the Hotel Coccumello, in what in ancient times had been a monastery. Two of the students in his party could play the piano and violin, and they were joined by musically talented friends from the Academy of Rome. They played American jazz and attracted business to the hotel.

The management was in an indulgent mood and let Grant use the lobby for a one-man exhibition of his paintings, some done in Paris and others in Sorrento. The paintings he sold at this exhibit, together with those he sold to subjects, provided enough money to pay for his trip. Some of his friends raised their eyebrows at his commercialism, but Grant had been painting to sell since grade school, and he continued to do so in France and in Italy. Usually he could sell the pictures he didn't want to bring back once he got them exhibited. "That to us was proof enough that Wood was no artist," the painter Rolf Armstrong once recalled. "No Frenchman or Italian ever wanted to buy the artistic sketches the rest of us made."

Grant had good luck getting subjects in Sorrento. The climate and scenery were what he had imagined as a boy when he read of sunny Italy and the blue Mediterranean. And though he spoke only a foreign tongue, he had never moved about more easily. Some of the natives were wood- and metalworkers, and they were pleased when he showed skill with these materials. People seemed willing to pose and to buy his pictures. "They were poor paintings," he said, "but my subjects seemed to like them. I sold them to people for whatever they could afford to pay."

One day he stopped in front of a pink stucco house. A woman came out on the portico and looked at him with understanding. She was willing to pose, and he began to sketch. She was a little on the buxom side, but comely, and her dark hair stood out well against the pink background. She watched him with interest, and seemed unconscious of herself. Grant thought he had seldom had a better model. Later, when he sold the painting, he learned that the pink stucco house was a *bordello*.

Life in Turner Alley

IN LATER years Grant was pictured as a man absorbed in Americana, deploring European influence, but he never tired of recalling that stay in Sorrento and the spring and summer that followed. He traveled to Palermo and Bordeaux, and through Brittany and Belgium, before returning to Paris, where he again fell in with spirited, free-living friends.

He hated to leave Paris, but his leave of absence was up and his money was beginning to run out. "The French are like kids; I like them," he said. One of his friends was a talented youth named Marcel Bordet, who spoke English well and knew all the twists in the city's night life. Grant was determined that Bordet should return to the United States with him and spoke to Ely, who visited Paris, about getting the Frenchman a job as a language teacher in America. But it couldn't be arranged, and Grant prepared to return home alone.

In his trunk, besides completed paintings, were a large number of sketches of French subjects, to be done in oil once he was back in Cedar Rapids. He was planning to have a Paris exhibition of his work as soon as he could finance it, and he made tentative arrangements with the Galerie Carmine, 51 Rue de Seine, for such a showing. So for the second time, when he sailed for America, he was planning still another trip to Paris.

In New York, he checked his goods through the customs and was leaning against a doorjamb, wondering how to get across town, when an official approached and asked where he was going.

"I want to go to Iowa, but I haven't got any money," Grant told him, thinking perhaps he was a taxi driver.

With his broad face, florid complexion, stocky build and sports shirt open at the neck, Grant could easily have been mistaken for a Bohemian farm hand. His expression was one of wonderment, and his slow speech suggested difficulty with the language. Iowa would be a natural place for him to be going—Czechoslovaks have settled in large numbers in the eastern part of the state. The official thought he got the idea.

He asked no more questions, but pinned an immigration tag on Grant and motioned sharply: "Right this way." There was no time for an explanation, so Grant picked up his luggage and followed along until he was among people who said "yah, yah" and spoke in some of the many languages he didn't understand. He attracted no particular attention and said nothing as he was herded with the immigrants into a bus and driven to a railroad station. When the crowded bus stopped, he stepped out, took his bearings, arranged for his trunk to be sent through, and got on a train—he had a coach ticket for Iowa.

Thus returned Cedar Rapids' foremost artist, after study abroad. His sister Nan had been married that summer to Edward E. Graham, and Grant gave her various presents from Paris. He brought his mother a cameo from Italy. Mrs. Wood looked long at her son; she was sixty-six years old, still well able to keep house for him, and glad of the chance to do it.

The paintings Grant brought back included *Italian Farmyard, The Blue Door, Fountain of the Medici,* and *Blue Vase, Sorrento.* He had sketches from which he finished *Oil Jar, Sorrento, Cottage, Brittany,* and *Street in Palermo.* There was little in them to suggest his later style.

His Paris wardrobe puzzled Mrs. Wood, and she finally gave to the neighbors several dozen gray Canton flannel shirts, full sleeved and of peasant length, that he never wore in Cedar Rapids. He had worn a beret in Paris, but this, too, he never put on at home. He went back to teaching at McKinley High School, this time at a salary of two hundred dollars a month.

79

Soon afterward he did his first work for David Turner, who became his chief sponsor. The Turners were moving their mortuary, established in 1888, to a new location, and they hired Grant to help decorate it. He made drawings of the entrance, entrance hall, reception room and façade, chose the furnishings, and hung his paintings on the mortuary walls. Turner, who had taken over active management from his father, John B., liked Grant's paintings, and liked having an artist around. He had an idea he could help promote Grant's career, and made him a proposal.

"Grant, why teach? I've got a steam-heated garage with a loft in it. You can live there."

Formerly a stable, the low and many-gabled garage sat on an alley behind the mortuary and was made of the same brick. Grant looked over what had been the old hayloft and decided he could make it into an apartment. Steam heat appealed to him. The move was made, and the Woods spent the next eleven years above the garage, with no rent to pay. The alley was nameless—no one else lived on it, and the garage had no number—but Grant always gave his address as 5 Turner Alley.

When it was said that they lived in a hayloft, people often pictured something out of one of the farm barns that Marvin Cone liked to paint, but it was scarcely that. The way Grant fixed it up, it was the kind of apartment that might rent, without any artistic or legendary connotations, for fifty or sixty dollars a month. Far from being obscure, it became a municipal attraction, one of the places to which distinguished visitors were likely to be taken.

Grant built an outside stairway, running down to the alley, and put a small kitchen and bathroom, with a sunken tub, where the inside stairwell had been. This left him a large room in which to paint, with light on his easel from the cupola, and dormer windows on either side. In one of the windows was a breakfast nook. Opposite the entrance was an alcove in which he and his mother slept, on beds that rolled away under the sloping roofs. Immediately to the right of the entrance was a storeroom, and to the left the small kitchen and bath.

He built in a small fireplace and used an overturned metal bushel as a cover for it. A teapot often sat on the upturned bottom of the bushel, and a Madonna statuette stood in a Gothic-style niche above it. Over the doors of a built-in bookcase, he stretched some of his old overalls, smeared them with plaster and painted them bronze. It gave a rough-antique effect to the doors from a distance, although on closer examination the outlines of pockets and patches in the overalls could be seen.

Grant's pupils pounded designs on flattened tobacco tins, and these were nailed as a facing onto a balustrade between the studio and the storeroom. The floor was roughly boarded, so he overlaid it with four-inch squares of wood enameled to resemble checkerboard tile. Then he made saucer-sized checker men with which a giant sort of checker game could be played on the floor.

He carved a pointed hand from wood, lettered "Grant Wood's Studio" on it, and nailed it to a telephone pole in the alley. At the foot of his stair he hung an old-fashioned farm lantern. On the glass of the front door he painted a clock arrangement and installed a revolving metal arrow. Around the edge of the clock was lettered: "Grant Wood Will Return to the Studio at—." The arrow could be pointed to the hour, or it could be pointed to "Is in," "Is out of town," "Is taking a bath," or "Is giving a party." He put a Parisian bell on springs so that it seemed to ring almost indefinitely when visitors pulled a cord.

Mrs. Wood braided a large, somber-colored rug for the studio floor. She filled the dormer windows with plants and flowers in boxes—snake plants, begonias, petunias, verbenas, geraniums, ferns and cacti—and had canned tomatoes, beans and corn sitting on various ledges about the place. Because of the sloping roofsides, there was only one good place to hang a picture, opposite the entrance, and Grant usually had his latest painting hanging there. He built rolling drawers in which to put others away.

The *Spotted Man*, too big for the drawers, stood in a corner. When the studio began to be a cultural gathering place, Miss Prescott gave Grant a square rosewood piano which visitors sometimes played. Grant became interested in flint glass, and several shelves of it, and some old carvings and knickknacks, were distributed around the studio. There were a few pieces of antique furniture, including Mrs. Wood's favorite rocking chair. At the high school, he had taught pupils to iron paraffin into ordinary wrapping paper and paint it for lamp shades—saving the cost of parchment—and some of these waxed-paper lamps lighted his studio.

Visiting lecturers, painters, writers, musicians and patrons of the arts were brought to the studio and served hot dogs, buns and coffee, tea or beer. Eastern, southern and midwestern dialects mingled. A dozen people were enough to crowd the studio, but there were sometimes many more, and there was a tendency to assume that everybody present was "doing something."

"What do you do, write, paint or what?" an eastern lady once asked archly while bending an eye on John Reid.

John Reid, president of the National Oats Company, had built a million-dollar business with three-minute cereals and the like, but he spoke in the tongue of Cedar Rapids and didn't like snobs.

"Who me?" he replied, putting an extra twang in his voice. "Why I run a grocery store down at Strawberry Point."

Visiting celebrities were comparatively rare, and more often the guests were local artistic talent—Marvin Cone, Leon Zeman, Arnold Pyle, Edgar Britton, and others—or people connected with the Cedar Rapids Little Gallery or the Community Theater.

Mrs. Wood sat back and watched it all, with a small, slightly apprehensive smile. In former years she would have hurried around trying to take care of guests, but she was getting too old for that now. She didn't say much, but nodded and smiled. The word visitors most often used to describe her was "quaint."

Grant's painting took a sensational turn for the first time after he moved to 5 Turner Alley. Although they hadn't yet shown in his work, he had come back from Paris with new ideas. His friends there had had a rich contempt for moralizing and restraint. Grant thought he should loosen up and break with tradition. The result was a brief series of paintings combining some of the worst features of the surrealists and the postwar neomeditationists. One of them was his impression of a piece of music and consisted of a number of concentric circles, some closed and some not, with tangents going this way and that, as he imagined the music went. The musical painting, done in brilliant colors, fell flat: not even Grant's best friends could say a good word for it. John Reid stood in front of it a long time, and then shook his head.

"Who's going to know what that thing is?"

Grant later strongly denounced this kind of painting, but at the time he lectured Reid at length on the importance of giving free play to the emotions and imagination, of getting moods and ideas on canvas before they escaped. Reid grumbled, parried and objected, and before long Grant was back at sober scenes. Then he had what he called a "palette-knife stage." He had experimented before at putting paint on with something besides brushes. One day at the Hansons, when they were living in the Kenwood woods, he found himself without brushes, waiting for Marvin Cone, who had been held up by the rain. Grant looked out of the window, put paint on a piece of Bristol board with his thumb, and did a fairly presentable rainy-day landscape.

Now he began putting on paint with a palette knife. One of his landscapes done in this fashion was so good that Reid insisted on paying him two hundred dollars for it. Grant was then getting twenty-five to forty dollars for his best work, with brushes, and was reluctant to take the money. Reid bought a second palette-knife product for fifty dollars and thought they were both well worth the money.

Grant's rent-free quarters made teaching at McKinley unnecessary, and he resigned after the 1924–25 term. Altogether he had taught for Miss Prescott five years, one of them part time.

He spent the summer of 1925 painting workers at the Cherry-Burrell dairy equipment manufacturing plant in Cedar Rapids. The workers at Cherry-Burrell became accustomed to seeing Grant with his easel in the plant day after day, and the studies in which he painted them showed no trace of posing. One of Barney Barnet, then seventy, almost told the story of his life: Barnet had been working at his trade for more than fifty years and his ability to make metal box covers remained high after his eyesight and hearing had begun to fail. Grant succeeded in picturing the efficiency still in the old man's hands, while age otherwise sat heavily upon him. He painted other studies strong in character—one of Jack Mejdle, taking an instrument reading, another of Joe Polehna, performing a turning operation on a gear, one of a spray painter, one of a goggled worker abrading a coil, and one of a youth putting arms on a shaft. These paintings never became well known.

The Cherry-Burrell portraits advanced through a series of sketches to the final drafts. Grant was inclined to take the long way around in everything he did. Frequently he made several sketches and then tried to combine into one the best features of each. His original sketches usually were small enough to go on an envelope, and his originals in color, small paintings themselves, weren't much bigger. He especially liked small, close work, and it might have been thought that miniatures would be exactly his field. Yet when he made wood-block miniatures of the graduating students at McKinley, he first drew them life size and then scaled them down. After completing the Cherry-Burrell work, he was commissioned to make two clay figures for the Church of the Immaculate Conception. He did these first in the nude, carefully outlining each saintly muscle. Then he covered them with ecclesiastical robes.

Although Grant didn't make much money during the first year after he gave up teaching, he was anxious to hold his Paris exhibition in 1926. He went to Ely in March and borrowed a thousand dollars which Ely didn't try to collect until sixteen years later when he took it without interest from the estate. Grant also borrowed from other sponsors, amounts they have forgotten, and sailed for Europe in April.

His paintings were on exhibit during June and July at the Galerie Carmine. There were forty-seven of them, all French in subject matter. Grant arrived in time for the Quat-z-Arts ball and this time managed to get in, wearing a ballet costume; but on the whole the trip lacked the carefree character of his previous stay in Paris. He was an artist this time, rather than a student, and as an exhibitor he was a fair mark for criticism.

Reid was in Paris that summer and had difficulty controlling his temper when rival painters, following their immemorial custom, dismissed Grant's work as small souled and insignificant. Even then Grant's slow and careful methods were criticized by those who thought the artist should express himself more freely.

"He's no artist," one of the visitors at the exhibit told Reid contemptuously.

"Why not?" Reid asked testily.

"You don't plan a picture. You go out into the country and look about until you feel an urge to paint"—and here the speaker's eyes glazed—"the thing that you see."

But such criticism from rivals and gallery-goers was to be expected. The Carmine was one of the smaller galleries of Paris, but considered very good, and Grant's exhibit was received favorably by the established critics. Pope Pius XI wrote to him expressing a desire to see more of his work and asked for reproductions of his paintings. It would have been possible for Grant to consider that he had achieved a gratifying artistic success.

However, he became depressed. No notice at all of his exhibit had been taken in the United States. He had sold some paintings, but not nearly enough to pay for his trip. No further Paris exhibit would be justified, even if it could be financed. All his life the pinnacle of his ambitions had centered in Paris; now he had had his Paris show and was just another fellow who had exhibited some paintings there. So when at the end of the summer he left Paris for the third time, he wasn't planning a future trip abroad.

He looked a long time at his mother when he reached 5 Turner Alley. She was wearing the cameo he had given her. The jagged braid of her apron formed a marching pattern around it. Her face had the weather-worn look of a woman who for months has seen nothing but endless prairie. It occurred to Grant that she was a better painting subject than anything he had seen in Europe, and he made a sketch of her the same day.

The idea was planted then, but in slow-growing soil. He didn't actually paint her portrait until three years later.

Renaissance in a Mortuary

DAVID TURNER started buying Grant's paintings to keep vacant places from appearing on his chapel and reception room walls. While the paintings were hanging there on exhibition, it was fine —fine for Turner and fine for Grant, who otherwise had no place to display his work. But every so often, when Dave was escorting a bereaved client, he would look up to find one of the paintings gone. This meant that Grant had sold it and the new owner had taken it away. So Dave bought the pictures to make sure they stayed put.

He kept on buying until he had forty-four of them, besides drawings and sketches. In addition, he sometimes bought a picture from some young artist in whom Grant was interested, from Nan, or from Marvin Cone, whose work he liked as well as Grant's.

At the same time, Turner recommended Grant as a painter and decorator. Some of the newspaper advertisements for the Turner Funeral Home dealt chiefly with Grant, urging subscribers to buy his pictures, extolling him as a credit to the community, and assuring that his paintings were a sound investment.

When the people of Cedar Rapids found that Dave Turner was sponsoring him, they did not ask for any better endorsement. Paul Hanson felt the rise in Grant's prestige, and asked him: "Why don't you charge three dollars an hour for your time? I'll bet you'd get it."

Grant demurred, but later settled on that figure and received three dollars an hour when he decorated house interiors for the Herbert Stamats, the Van Vechten Shaffers and other Cedar Rapids families.

Turner didn't confine his efforts to Cedar Rapids but talked Grant Wood wherever he went. At the conventions of the National Selected Morticians Association, he maneuvered himself each year onto the committee to buy a present for the president, then saw to it that the present was a Grant Wood painting. He also got Grant on the speaking program at one of the conventions, as an expert in interior decorating.

Grant told the delegates how to make a short room look long or a low room tall, how to warm a cold room with the colors of flame, how to use mellow lighting, how to salvage old furniture, and how to get a rich effect by hanging good paintings on the walls. "Beware of chromos and cheap and ordinary prints," he advised. "Better have a plain wall than tinted photographs. Substitute simple landscapes for cupids with arrows and damsels at fountains."

The talk to the funeral directors went over well. Publicity concerning 5 Turner Alley seemed to be having an effect. Turner and Grant began to imagine a whole row of studios along the alley. It was to be an artists' colony, the "Greenwich Village of the Corn Belt," with "the only truly Bohemian atmosphere west of Hoboken." Reporters were called in to hear of the plan, and devout people worried about the morals of the unborn colony. Grant felt it necessary to assure them that its activities would not "reach the lurid heights ascribed to communities of artists," and that "good taste will be the first requirement of the residents of Turner Alley."

What was called the Fine Arts Studio Group was formed in the fall of 1926 to carry the project through. It had fifteen artists and musicians on its board of directors, and listed its patrons as Turner, Reid, Ely and a publisher, J. S. Farquhar—an impressive array of financial backing.

Yet no part of the project was carried through. Not a stone was laid, and Turner Alley, only two blocks long and exceptionally narrow, remained almost unadorned. A few hollyhocks, zinnias and sunflowers grew along the back fences, and tall trees rose to embrace decrepit two-story barns, but the alley's only claim to fame was the low brick stable where Grant had his studio.

One thing did grow indirectly out of the plans for a Cedar Rapids Latin Quarter. The three-story Edward O. Mansfield home was taken over and established as a cultural center. The Hobby House, a gift shop operated by Mary Lackersteen and Hazel Brown, and Don Horan's music studio were on the first floor; the art school of the Cedar Rapids Art Association, with Leon Zeman in charge, and the "blue pencil" room of Jean C. Herrick, city editor of the *Cedar Rapids Republican*, took up the second story, and Edgar Britton had an artist's studio on the third floor.

Grant was a regular visitor at the Hobby House, as the entire establishment was usually known. He tried out his ideas on whatever artistic talent was gathered. Standing with his feet apart, his arms folded, a cigarette between two fingers, he would begin his conversation on a high note and let his voice fall.

"I've got an idea," he would say. He explained in detail there his plans for *American Gothic, Arnold Comes of Age,* and *Victorian Survival.* Although he often didn't act on his ideas for years, if at all, he never seemed afraid that they would be stolen. He sought out people who would listen to them.

Sometimes he called Reid out of bed at two or three o'clock in the morning to join him at an all-night lunch counter near the interurban station and listen to his latest idea. Reid didn't object; he had made a lot of money, but nothing appealed to him as more worthwhile than his friendship for Grant. They usually ate hot dogs or chili at such sessions. They especially liked chili, and on one occasion, when both were in St. Louis, spent half a night combing the city for a good sample of it. Grant kept reproaching Reid: "You ought to know where there's good chili here. For goodness sake, you were born and raised here."

Grant also had some fancy eating habits, for suitable occasions. He had learned in Paris to mix his own salad, after consecrating the bowl with a piece of garlic. He helped organize a Garlic Club which held forth each noon in a corner of the Travel Inn. Mac-Kinlay Kantor, a Cedar Rapids product, was a member of it. Ed Wynn was taken in as an honorary member. Reid and Farquhar often attended. Regulars included Grant, Ralph Leo, Helen Mc-Laughery Taylor, Marvin Cone, Betty Low, Don Ferron, Tex Grantham, Mrs. Burgess West, Russell Landstrom, and Ted Seely. These were well-known people in Cedar Rapids. Talent, intellect, the press and money were well represented. Grant had come a long way since the days of his first experience with newspapers, when he tried to sell them a hoax after fishing the iron kettle from Cook's Pond. Through the Garlic Club he became a contributor to a newspaper column.

Grantham conducted a column called "The Hell Box" in the *Cedar Rapids Republican*. Grant and other members of the club sent contributions to it. When in 1926 Grantham left for another job, "The Hell Box" was turned over to a group known as "The Seven Seers," each of whom was to write a column a week. Grant was one of the seers. He used his space to attack the outdoor advertising that was cluttering up the scenery around Cedar Rapids. It had been stipulated that the seers could write anything they chose, and Grant named some of the offending advertisers in his denunciations. The result was unfortunate: the offenders, while continuing their outdoor display, withdrew advertising from the *Republican*. The weight of advertising had already shifted to the *Gazette*, and early the following year, in 1927, it absorbed the *Republican*.

Grant's prestige continued to grow. Young artists looked at him in those days and wondered if they, too, would become successful. He wore a raccoon coat and was in the public eye. He was identified with liberal groups, read Mencken and the better art magazines, and was called on for opinions and comments. Plenty of girls would have liked to keep house for him, but Grant didn't follow up his opportunities. He spoke seriously of the matter to Vida and seemed puzzled about himself.

"I guess I'm just not interested in women," he said.

To him, his life didn't seem glamorous. From the Paris point of view, he was living in a small town. Members of the Garlic Club scattered, and stories of their successes in various other parts of the country floated back to Cedar Rapids, while he went on painting and decorating. Hazel and Mary managed a tearoom for a while, exhibited his paintings in it, and sold some for as high as two hundred dollars—these were better prices than he could ordinarily hope for.

He clung to his old habits and ideas. Some people said he had made a fetish of being odd. He wore ordinary farmers' overalls to work and paint in, and would wear nothing else; the lines and seams of a pair of overalls had a kind of fascination for him. He continued to insist that everything be done with the least possible expense: his treatment for old furniture was to wash it with soap and water, and when the Turners wanted to panel one of the rooms in their home he got the desired effect by nailing painted screen-door stripping over the wallpaper. He still gathered pieces of junk, and when he needed something in metal, frequently made it himself at a forge he kept outside No. 5.

Above all, he held to his slow habits of work. Social events in Cedar Rapids are well spaced; his evenings were usually free, and he kept no regular hours. He could and frequently did stay up all night to work at his easel at 5 Turner Alley. He still never hurried, and his time was his own.

Window in Europe

His time was his own, but not without a struggle. People sometimes complained that if a man wasn't right up his alley, Grant
didn't have any use for him. That wasn't entirely true: he spent
hours talking to the Danish farmer along the route to Cook's Pond
and to a little inconspicuous janitor-engineer at the school. But
it was true that brisk, ambitious people annoyed him, and nothing
was more complete than the unconcern with which he ignored
them.

He had a way of acting hopelessly stupid in order to avoid doing
something he didn't want to do. If pressed he flatly refused. He
never joined any nonartistic organization except the American
Legion, and he joined that at Anamosa, thirty miles away, where
he seldom went, instead of at Cedar Rapids, where it might have
taken up some of his time. After they were living on Turner Alley,
the Reverend William M. Evans approached the Woods about
attending his church, the Central Park Presbyterian. Grant
"didn't seem interested."

Yet he was always available for any community project that
was in his field. The Cedar Rapids Art Association and the Little
Gallery had his active support. He made a series of drawings of
old things in Cedar Rapids that might be forgotten—the "steam
motor" to nearby Marion; a wood-burning fire engine that had
been used by volunteers; "Little Muddy," the settlement's first
church; the first trading post. And at the beginning of 1927, he
applied for and was granted a commission to make a large
stained-glass window for the projected Cedar Rapids Memorial
Building and City Hall.

The window proved one of the most discouraging things he had undertaken. In applying for the commission he said it would take at least a year to complete the job, and that was an underestimate. It absorbed much of his energy for the next two years, took him on his fourth trip to Europe, brought him little money and only the satisfaction of the trip in exchange.

His application was dated December 24, 1926, and on January 25, 1927, he was granted nine thousand dollars for the job. On March 30, he was given a formal contract for ten thousand dollars, with one thousand reserved for the cost of framing, installation and glass. The window was to be twenty feet wide, twenty-four feet high and in fifty-eight sections—the "largest stained-glass window in the world."

Grant's color sketch showed a twelve-foot central figure of a woman in Grecian robes of lavender with a pale rose cast, representing the Heroic Republic, and holding the palm branch of Peace in her right hand and the laurel of Victory in her left. She stood against an amber sky with her feet pointed downward in clouds. Below her, on either side of a central stone, were six life-sized figures of fighting men of the country's various wars.

The figures of the soldiers gave him the most trouble. He particularly liked to paint and emphasize individual characteristics, and was never really satisfied that he knew a face until he had seen it a great many times. His sister Nan, his mother, his dentist, his protégé Arnold Pyle, Winifred Cone and Marvin, and Paul and Vida were the kinds of models with whom he did his best work. But it was essential that the veterans be typical. In Grant's view, a typical person was a person who did not even exist: it was an average of several people or someone close to the average with his individuality painted under. Nan, who posed for her brother more times than she can remember, posed again for the central figure, and it turned out well. The sketches of the veterans dragged on for months.

Grant didn't give all his time to the work; he did various painting and decorating jobs, spent a vacation painting at Waubeek,
a little town on the Wapsipinicon River, and several times visited
Stone City, also on the Wapsie. But he was often seen in the
streets of Cedar Rapids, peering into the faces of strangers for
features he could use on the window. Models to suit him were
finally found, and on January 18, 1928, almost a year after he had
undertaken the work, his sketch was approved by the Memorial
Window Commission.

Staining glass was largely a European industry. It was thought
to be almost out of the question to get the work on this huge window done in the United States. The best craftsmen for the job
were in Germany, at Munich. Yet it was realized that there might
be some objection to having a veterans' memorial done in the
country of a late enemy. In an attempt to save Grant from being
blamed, a resolution was pushed through stating "it is the sense of
the commission that there is no objection to the work's being
done in Germany." A contract was let to the Frei Art Glass Company, a St. Louis firm that could arrange for the staining in
Munich.

Grant prepared to go abroad. While arrangements were being
made, he painted *Quilts*, *Midsummer*, and *Red Bedding*. He
painted murals for "corn rooms" in hotels at Cedar Rapids and
Council Bluffs. In the late summer and early fall, he was at Waubeek again. Jay Sigmund, Cedar Rapids insurance man and poet,
was there with him. Grant's painting was beginning to show strong
indications of his later style. His corn shocks fell into regular rows
and gave a feeling of space and desolation. He liked to paint
around 4:00 P. M., when the shadows helped him lay the ground
down—lay it down and then lift it up again, swelling and billowing almost to the top of the canvas.

In late September he left for Germany. His troubles with the window were only begun. In Munich, he had ten to twelve trained workmen under him to stain it, but the workmen were accustomed to dealing with religious subjects. When his soldiers were transferred to the glass, they looked like uniformed saints. They had pinched noses and the small nostrils of Gothic art. They lacked independent carriage and the typical bony structure he had given their faces. The bearded Civil War soldier looked like a conception of Christ.

Grant decided to do the staining himself. The work was done on bits of antique glass, fastened to a plate glass with wax. Detail was applied with an iron oxide paint, and the glass was then placed in a frame and fired. The faces looked clear enough as Grant first applied the paint, but when they were fired the features faded out. He applied heavier paint and the glass blistered.

He finally did all the faces except that of the World War soldier, which was put onto the glass by Emil Frei, who also went to Munich for the work. The workmen ran into difficulty with the body of the figure for the War of 1812, a sailor stripped to the waist; in their first few attempts his skin was either so light that it formed a white spot in the window or so dark that he didn't look like a white man.

Then a controversy arose over Grant's abbreviated use of Roman numerals. He had shortened them to get them into the spaces under the figures—for 1898 he had MCCMIIC instead of MDCCCXCVIII or MDCCCLXXXXVIII. The controversy was finally carried to the University of Munich, where his version was held "unusual but technically justified."

The delays were enough to exasperate a more excitable person. Grant took them calmly. He was not a man to stand over workmen or to try to push ahead. He came, he looked at what was being done, he offered bland objections, and went out. He wandered through Munich's museums and art galleries, and was especially impressed by the works of fifteenth- and sixteenth-century German and Flemish painters.

He was thirty-seven years old, almost thirty-eight. He was an old hand at exhibiting, and had studied how to attract attention with color, arrangement and design. He knew the choice spots in the exhibit halls and had noticed, and deplored, the way strange and spectacular pictures ran away with the shows.

He could not help but think how one of these old Flemish paintings would stand out if placed among the vague, fuzzy things that artists were then doing. Those bony faces of Hans Memling's, the severe poses, the hard lines, staring eyes, intense expressions, perhaps done in lighter colors so as not to look too archaic, and set in some strong design—these were things well calculated to leap out at the critics, buyers and gallery-goers, if only because of their sharp contrast with the sort of painting that was being done.

Moreover, the German and Flemish primitives were the kind of thing Grant liked to do. They were not created by men who slashed on paint during bursts of emotion. They were made by deliberate, careful men who worked long with small brushes, men who had feeling for small details as well as for over-all effect. It occurred to him in Munich that he could get some of the primitive effect into his painting, and he studied the methods used by the old masters.

The glazing technique of renaissance painters attracted him. He stood long in the Old Pinakothek watching a copyist who was using this method. It was once practiced throughout Europe by men to whom time and pains apparently meant nothing. They laid on paint in varnished layers, and each layer was sufficiently translucent to let some of the paint beneath it show through. It gave their pictures depth and an oily appearance that cannot be obtained otherwise.

The method was not new to Grant. He had tried for translucent

STONE CITY

AMERICAN GOTHIC

mixtures when he had nothing better to work with than barn paint, egg whites and strained honey. But the effectiveness of it struck him in Munich, and he considered whether or not he could use it. He had plenty of time to think, since he spoke no German and could find few people who spoke English. He carried a pad like a deaf-mute, and drew pictures to make himself understood.

He did learn a few German words, two of them, for light and dark, in connection with the work on the window. He added one or two more words so he could tell a story.

"I went into a restaurant alone and ordered a glass of beer," he would say. "I said 'beer,' and the waitress easily understood me. I was somewhat astonished when she looked at me and said: 'Hell.' I said nothing, and she brought me light beer.

"When I got up to leave, I dropped the usual tip on the table. As I turned to go, I distinctly heard the waitress say: 'Donkey.' They were the only two English words I had heard spoken in some time, and neither was complimentary. I remarked on the incident to Mr. Frei, and when he stopped laughing he cleared things up.

" 'Hell' was the German word for light and what I understood as 'donkey' was short for 'dankeschoen,' the German thank you."

The window gave Grant one more bad turn before he left Munich. When it was virtually completed and laid out for examination, he realized that its border of army, navy and marine insignia was too small for such a large window.

Frei saw this too, but to re-do the border at this stage involved considerable expense, and neither he nor Grant said anything for several days. They went about avoiding each other's glance until each understood so well what the other was thinking that Frei broke into the middle of the subject.

"All right," he said, "if you'll redesign the border we'll do it over."

The redesign was completed, and Grant returned to Cedar Rapids at the end of 1928. The window was not well received. Members of the American Legion and the Daughters of the American Revolution denounced its having been done in Germany. People said that the hall in front of it wasn't long enough to give an effective view, that there was nothing on either side to set it off, and that it didn't look like anything from the outside. There was praise for it, too, but not enough to smother the protests.

It was better appreciated years later, when the second World War was on. Women and sometimes men came and stood long before it, abashed to be found staring and yet reluctant to leave. They got something from the tall Grecian woman with her downcast eyes, and from the rough soldier figures beneath her, that brought them a measure of comfort to sustain them in their loss. But that was long afterward.

As months passed and nothing was done to give the window a proper reception, Grant became disturbed. On May 11, 1929, he wrote an appealing letter to the Memorial Window commissioners, urging them to complete the plans that had been made. With almost a touch of anguish, he told them that the window would not appear finished until a proper inscription had been placed on the central stone, that he had hoped the window would be given a public unveiling, that he was sure the community would benefit from such a ceremony, and suggested frankly that he might gain by it, too.

Criticism of the window had reached a point where the Legion asked him to state his case; and then it seemed to die down. But the members of the commission decided to let sleeping dogs lie. The farthest they would go was to pass a resolution stating that Grant had "completed a satisfactory installation." To this day there is no inscription on the central stone, and no dedication ceremony ever was held.

FOURTEEN

Two Old Maps

WHEN Grant first returned from Munich, he was still interested in windows. He persuaded Dave Turner to let him put one in the mortuary, and this second window, covered with vines, now sheds a mellow light in changing colors on the rostrum of the Turner chapel.

By the time the chapel window was completed, it had become clear that the big window wasn't going to cause the sensation Grant had hoped it would. It was a disappointment, and he lost all desire ever to look at a stained-glass window again. He went back to painting.

The 1929 boom was on. People with money for the arts were getting rich, or richer. Success was so common that only large amounts of it interested anybody. A golden flow of dollars seemed to have been unloosed.

Except for the fact that he had a place to live, Grant wasn't much better off financially than he had been in his darkest days. His commissions for two years' work on the window amounted to less than eight hundred dollars, and his other income had dwindled during the period. Though the market was ripe, he had nothing to sell.

But he still had his ability to concentrate on detail, and he had new ideas that were putting this ability to better use. There in his low-gabled studio on the edge of the alley, far back from Second Avenue, he was concentrating as never before, and what had formerly gone into junk flowers, models and gadgets now went into his painting. More ideas came to him than he could hope to deal with. For the first time, he felt that material was all around him. The people he knew, the fields, the fence posts, Stone City, the jungle-bordered Wapsie, and the farm buildings all seemed worth painting. He brought out an old map, which he had had for several years, and got an idea from that.

The map had been on his mind for seven or eight years. He had seen it in a farmhouse and was attracted to it, but at first did nothing about acquiring it. It was an ordinary old-fashioned map of Iowa done in browns and greens with some symbolic horses, old mansions and various designs worked in unobtrusively in a style that was once common. He could hardly say what attracted him, but its fascination for him seemed to grow.

He kept thinking about it. He heard that the farmer's wife had died and that the farmer wasn't much of a housekeeper. That worried him. Perhaps mice were nibbling at the edges of the map. Perhaps rain was blowing through a window on it. Perhaps it would be thrown away.

Grant finally called Paul Hanson, and Paul drove him to the farmhouse. They got the map for next to nothing, and Grant gingerly loaded it into the car as though it were an old masterpiece. On the drive back to Cedar Rapids, Grant talked about the map. He had vague thoughts of using it in a painting sometime, but he had no definite idea; his immediate object was to get it and keep it safe.

He put the map in his canvas drawer, and there it remained for years. Sometimes he got it out to show to people and seemed puzzled that they weren't as impressed as he was. In the course of four or five years, almost everybody except himself forgot he had it.

After looking into Memling's faces at Munich, he became eager to do a portrait, something strong in character as Memling had done. And he came to a decision that must have been difficult for an artist who had had a one-man exhibit in Paris and who knew only too well how artists there would sneer at such a backwoods display—to enter the competition of the Iowa State Fair in Des Moines.

A pioneer subject would be appropriate, and the old map of Iowa a suitable background. He selected John B. Turner, Dave's father, for a portrait, and persuaded him to pose for *John B. Turner—Pioneer.*

The elder Turner, at seventy-one, was a product of the more robust days of Cedar Rapids. A Republican, he had carried on a historic feud with the *Gazette*, which, now Independent, was Democratic and under the guidance of the late Fred Faulkes.

Turner's mortuary was located near the *Gazette* office, and their political rivalry often took spectacular forms. For a while they were content with sniping at each other and with such tricks as sending German bands to play indefinitely in front of each other's establishments.

Faulkes decided to go beyond such picayune annoyance. He arranged a telephone call in which a voice told Turner that a corpse was sprawled out on an island in the Cedar River. Turner called the coroner and together they raced down to the riverbank opposite the island.

As they expected, they saw the body of a man lying on the island. They ran down along the river until they found a rowboat, and they rowed madly back. After all, the man might still be alive. When they got to the island, all they found was a pair of overalls and a shirt, stuffed with straw and topped by an old hat.

When the victims realized what had happened, they glanced up and saw half the *Gazette's* staff and a good number of other townspeople watching from the riverbank. Jeers, catcalls, guffaws and convulsed laughter greeted them as they rowed sheepishly back. Turner's position was bad; it was extremely embarrassing for a funeral director to be reported as rushing about in search, especially a fruitless search, of a corpse.

Time passed and the story wore thin. Then Turner had his inning. The funeral director waited until the last day of a mayoralty campaign. His candidate was a Republican named Connor; the *Gazette* was frantically backing a Democrat named Huston.

In those days an afternoon newspaper was just that—an afternoon newspaper. It didn't, as papers do today, keep a staff down until late at night, getting out street editions, predate editions or country-mail editions. When the *Gazette* rolled off the presses at 4:00 P. M., everybody went home and the place was locked up.

Turner was well aware of this practice, and he had a huge cloth streamer made, "CONNOR FOR MAYOR," that would stretch clear across the Gazette Building. After the paper closed, the day before the election, he and his men raised ladders against the offices of the *Gazette* and nailed the sign into place.

People in the streets looked at the sign in consternation. Connor for mayor? Wasn't the *Gazette* backing Huston? The news spread from man to man and woman to woman, faster than printed word could have carried it.

Certain executives left late dinner tables to tear down the sign, and efforts were made to reassure the voters that Huston had the *Gazette's* backing. But prosaic truth was brushed aside, while the sensation traveled fast and far. By the next day it was all over town, and would not be downed, that the *Gazette* had turned at the last minute. Turner's candidate was elected.

Something of that spirit was what Grant sought to capture in *John B. Turner—Pioneer*. It showed in the old man's square, seamed face—tough, challenging, almost sardonic on the surface, yet with a sly humor and a good appetite for living showing through.

As Grant reproduced it, from several sketches, the expression was one of those for which any adjective is wrong. The old man certainly looked unbeaten and unbowed; still, it isn't easy to be retired and shelved and ready to leave a city you helped build and where you once figured as one of the strongest. That, too, showed in the portrait.

Dave Turner says: "To me, that isn't a portrait of my father; that *is* my father." It was Grant's ambition to make his portraits, as he put it, "more like the subjects than the subjects themselves," and he no doubt achieved his aim in this, his first great portrait, by fusing into one expression what John Turner had been at different times in a long life. From the day it was completed, no one looked at the painting with indifference.

Plans for several other paintings were turning over in Grant's head as he worked on the Turner portrait. *Woman with Plants*, *Stone City*, and *American Gothic* were in the making; he had decided to use the glazing technique and was getting paints and making tests for the purpose.

But he was not in a position to refuse paying work. When the Turner portrait was done, he painted murals for another "corn room" in a Sioux City hotel. Then he took work as a decorator for Van Vechten Shaffer, a Cedar Rapids banker who was furnishing a new home.

At the Shaffers', Grant spent six months painting the panels of a pair of double doors. He used small brushes to paint medallion-sized heads and figures and seemed endlessly absorbed. Mrs. Shaffer almost gave up hope that the doors would ever be finished.

When the decorating was finally completed, Grant said he wanted to do portraits of the two little Shaffer girls, Mary Van Vechten and Susan Angevine, who had been watching him at his work. The reason he gave was that both had heads of long, heavy hair, which presented a painting problem that interested him. He asked $150 apiece, his regular price for portraits. Mrs. Shaffer agreed.

At his studio, Grant was working on *Woman with Plants*, the portrait of his mother. He was using the glazing method exclusively now. Slow and tedious as this may have seemed to most artists, it appealed to Grant's taste. The fact that it involved seven or eight coats of paint, besides coats of varnish, was an advantage: he enjoyed the physical act of putting on paint.

There were technical problems that could not be solved to his complete satisfaction. The exact mixture of paints used by the old masters was not known and could only be approximated. He could not allow the long periods for drying each coat of paint that was common practice four hundred years before. Titian let some of his coats of paint dry for as long as six months—too slow a process in modern times even for a painter of Grant's pace.

His mother was seventy-one years old and somewhat ill. She kept falling asleep while she posed. There had been better occasions, during the years he had had it in mind, to use her as a painting subject. But Grant kept on with the work. When he was concentrating on a painting, he could be almost oblivious to the plight of his models: once when Marvin's wife Winifred Cone was posing for him, he suddenly flashed a strong light in her face, and she fainted; Grant didn't seem greatly disturbed.

Mrs. Wood didn't have to pose for long periods. Grant didn't require much posing but spent most of his painting time looking at what was on his easel, swaying slowly from one foot to the other. "The model is only the bones," he once said. "I really paint what I see in my head."

He had a strange notion that what he was painting would never be known as a portrait of his mother. He thought he was altering, pointing up, not making it especially recognizable. What was to become the best-known mother portrait of its day started out to be merely a woman of the plains. Had he intended it to represent a portrait of his mother, he could hardly have given it that hollow, cold, objective title: *Woman with Plants*.

During the summer of 1929, Grant made a trip to Eldon, a little town in Wapello County in the southern part of Iowa. Edward Rowan, who was in charge of the Carnegie-financed Little Gallery in Cedar Rapids and who carried on projects elsewhere as well, had him come down there to give a sketching exhibition.

As Grant walked along a street in Eldon he saw a small frame house with a Gothic-style window above its full-length porch. He said, "That's the house I've been looking for," and made a color sketch of it on the spot. He also had a photograph taken of it. It was the house he used in the background of *American Gothic*. A little later he made his first sketch for *Stone City*. In the wake of his enormous window, he was having one of the most fertile creative periods ever realized by an artist.

That same summer his portrait of Turner was on exhibition at the Iowa Fair. With the map in the background behind the elderly Turner's face, it was sometimes known as "Two Old Maps." It won the portrait and sweepstakes prizes. The judge, Oskar Gross, a Chicago critic and portrait painter, said: "I haven't seen anything like this since the old Dutch masters. Surely a young man could not have painted it."

FIFTEEN

Portraits That Lived

Mrs. Wood belonged to a generation that saw more changes than any generation had seen before. She was seven years old when her parents brought her across the Iowa prairie in a covered wagon to homestead near Anamosa on some of the earth's richest soil. Not all of Iowa is fertile: the dingy homes and sagging barns of hilly southern sections tell a different story. The Weavers, however, got land in a belt stretching from the southeast to the north-central part of the state, above which the glaciers stopped and where the ground for the most part rises and falls like a swelling but unbroken sea.

The belt contains the blackest of the black soil for which Iowa is famous, and the people who settled it prospered. Members of Hattie Weaver's generation didn't have to be told that the future was theirs; it could be seen all around them. Railroads were being brought through, towns and cities were springing up, and huge farmhouses, mansions really, were being built. Lean steers were brought from western ranges to be fed from cornfields that regularly turned out fifty to a hundred bushels an acre, and tall silos, huge barns, fat hogs and fatter cattle took their places in the landscape.

It was natural to wait for still bigger things to happen. Hattie Weaver was in no hurry to marry. She taught the primary grades; she never put herself forward; she saved her money from year to year. She was twenty-eight years old when she married Maryville Wood and went with him to set up housekeeping on his farm, and though her age appeared on Grant's birth certificate as the conventional twenty-nine, she was nearly thirty-three when he was born. She was past forty when Nan came. Maryville died the following year.

A new series of changes occurred during the years she spent stretching the estate until she was deeply in debt, during the years she lived with Grant and waited for grandchildren that never came. By the time Grant painted her portrait, traffic jams in Cedar Rapids were a problem and paved highways dipped and curved in every direction, on the route to Anamosa and over the old trail on which her father had carried a rifle to protect them from Indians.

Mrs. Wood probably spent little time puzzling over the course of events. If knowledge has depth as well as breadth, farming people know as much as anybody else, maybe more. But it is true that most of them dislike broad concepts and think in simple terms. Mrs. Wood was that kind: she saw the changes; she did not try to fathom them. Whatever happened was a part of the world, as natural as being alive. It was enough to find out what she and her children should do.

If Grant wanted her to pose, she was anxious to do it, and to do it well. There is just a trace of that eagerness in the portrait, and there is much more. Grant's problem was to call back those years over which her mind wandered, not with thousand-league paces but with everyday steps—to make the portrait speak of prairies and hard winters and disappointments and courage; to make the person seem greater than the land. It was all there in her worn, weathered face; probably he didn't realize how much of her he got into it.

He dropped his background down to give an effect of great space—an old style, used by Leonardo in *Mona Lisa*. He even had a small road winding there far below, as in *Mona Lisa*. A phalanx of corn shocks moved on a red schoolhouse, set on somewhat higher ground, and a row of mushroom-shaped trees led to a windmill fixed in the distance. Mrs. Wood wore the apron with the jagged braid that had impressed him three years before, and the cameo he had brought her from Italy. An old-fashioned, big-leafed begonia sat by her right hand, and she held a potted snake-plant in her lap.

The snakeplant (Sansevieria) is one of the most hardy of growths, suggesting solitude and desolation, though probably that was not Grant's reason for selecting it. He was thinking in terms of design and needed something straight up and down. The tall snakeplant, sometimes called widow's tongue or mother-in-law's tongue, and her left arm brought straight across to hold it strengthened a design that otherwise would have shown too many curves and ovals. And he had seen that snakeplant for years; he knew exactly how to paint it.

The portrait was only 20½ by 17½ inches. It was made to hang in a house. Its lighting was uniform, as on a slightly over-cast day, and every detail was brought out. Grant worked late hours over it. When a coat of glaze was dry he went over it with a safety-razor blade until it was as smooth as glass before applying the next coat. Sometimes people suggested that he could have found something better than a razor blade for the purpose, but he insisted that "there's nothing better for it in the world."

Grant didn't like the painting when it was done. He took a photograph of his mother to Clarabelle Weaver and asked her to hang it in her room in place of a print of the portrait. He said he hadn't meant the portrait to represent his mother and didn't want Clarabelle to remember her that way.

The photograph showed Mrs. Wood with a small, self-conscious smile. It had no story to tell, except that she was having her picture taken. That Grant actually preferred it to the portrait is almost beyond belief, yet the same photograph stood on his mantel the rest of his life. Perhaps the plumbing shows too much when artists look at their own pictures. Perhaps Grant suffered too much over the details to be able to forgive the finished product. Or it may have been because to the story of her past there was the present tragedy to be added: that she was old and anxious, near the end of her life.

To Frank Wood the portrait seemed more like their mother than any photograph could be, and to him nothing pictured her with more sympathy and understanding. Nan, like Grant, preferred a photograph. Nan felt that even the fact that her mother was then ill showed in the portrait, and her eyes seemed to be looking out for a last glimpse of what could not be brought back—it was too sad.

He was still looking for more close detail when he turned from the portrait of his mother to the portraits of the Shaffer girls. Around Mary Van Vechten Shaffer's neck he put a wide collar of Irish lace, intricate in pattern, and in Susan Angevine Shaffer's hand he placed a delicate sprig of fleabane (erigeron). Mrs. Shaffer had specified that the portraits should have no backgrounds, and Grant agreed to that. The Flemish masters had also sometimes done portraits without backgrounds.

Though originally he had asked to do the girls' portraits because of their hair, he put a lace-patterned bonnet on Susan when he came to paint her. During the period when he was decorating the Shaffer home the girls had plied him with questions as he worked, and Susan had been especially insistent on getting the right answers. So in the portrait he gave her a pugnacious expression—she is probably the most pugnacious little girl in painting. He was also thinking of the contrast with the delicate sprig of fleabane, which seemed unlikely to survive long in her hands.

Mrs. Shaffer was well satisfied with the portrait of Susan, but she didn't like the one of Mary so well. She wanted Grant to put a line in at the base of her forehead, or something to give Mary a little more expression. Grant wouldn't do it, not for anybody; when he was through with a painting, he was through with it for good.

The appearance of *Woman with Plants* didn't cause any particular sensation. It was shown at the Art Institute exhibit in the fall of 1929, didn't win a prize, and was bought by the Cedar Rapids Art Association for three hundred dollars. The critics discovered Grant a year later, and then not for *Woman with Plants* but for *American Gothic*. It was only after several years that Mrs. Wood's portrait came to be called "the first masterpiece of the American school," and to be compared with Whistler's portrait of his mother.

The comparison is difficult to see. From an artistic standpoint there is more contrast than comparison, and the subjects themselves represent entirely different types. Mrs. Wood, with her strong forehead, broad face and broad straight mouth, was a plain woman; Whistler's mother appears as a woman of gentle breeding. Somehow it is all implicit in the portrait: that Mrs. Wood had stood on a wind-swept hill in an unsettled country, had hunted elderberries through the hazel brush, had seen her home sold under a sheriff's hammer.

Because so many people were disturbed by the fact that Mrs. Wood was holding only one snakeplant, the portrait was often called "Woman with Plant." Grant had in mind the begonia, too, though it was a little obscure there at her side. He called it *Woman with Plants* in a note he later put in his own handwriting on the back of the painting. The note read: "This picture, 'Woman with Plants,' was damaged by fire in 1929. It has been restored and is protected by being sealed, air tight, against dust. Please do not break seal. Grant Wood."

The truth was considerably "stylized" in that note. The only fire that occurred was in an electric heater which, along with an electric fan, he turned on the portrait to speed the drying of the paint. Possibly the damage was caused by the heater, or the fan, or something in the paint, or, most probable of all, by the fact that the paint simply wasn't given enough time to dry. And it wasn't sealed primarily against dust, but against air, to stop further drying.

Grant found the glazing method a tricky thing to handle. Titian did not let coats of paint dry six months for nothing. If each coat of paint wasn't completely dry before the next was applied, they would dry unevenly and cause blistering. That was what happened to *Woman with Plants*. The same thing happened to Susan's portrait, which also was restored. *American Gothic* remained in good shape, but was kept under glass. His later paintings, using the same method, held up better.

By the end of 1929, Grant had completed three portraits that would have to be included in any list of his dozen best works—Turner, his mother, and Susan. Yet there was still no general opinion, even in Cedar Rapids, that he was anything more than a fairly successful artist—if that. Soon after he had worked for them, the Shaffers wanted a family portrait copied; Mr. Shaffer didn't think Grant was a good enough painter to do the job.

Thirty-five Cents an Acre

GRANT's favorite play was George Bernard Shaw's *Androcles and the Lion*. The subject of the drama could hardly come up without his suggesting that it be produced. He even read and reread Shaw's long, discursive preface, which contains enough heresies to shock every Presbyterian in Cedar Rapids. Reid often joked with him about his fondness for the play. If they entered a large room, Reid would say: "Well, do you think this is big enough to put on *Androcles and the Lion?*"

A Community Theater project was launched in Cedar Rapids late in 1929. The first play, at Grant's suggestion, was put on in his studio. It was *Androcles and the Lion*. The lists of community plays that have been given do not include it now, and people recall it only as one of Grant Wood's brainstorms, but Grant always contended that the Community Theater was born there in his studio and that its first attempt was more successful than any of the plays that followed.

He made a shaggy headpiece with jaws that opened and closed, and a set of paws and a tail, to wear as the lion. He practiced blood-curdling roars, wails of pain and whimperings of affection. The small audience, hardly bigger than the cast, was convulsed, and even the actors had to take time out to laugh.

The official Community Theater got under way soon afterward. Tearooms were taken over for such plays as *Journey's End, Queen's Husband, Dover Road, The Last Mile,* and *Outward Bound*. Grant was a prime mover in these productions, building and painting scenery and sometimes taking a part in a play. When they gave *The Queen's Husband*, he took the part of the king's secretary and wore a peaked helmet during a disturbance at the palace. No helmet large enough for him could be found, and the one he wore sat on top of his head and teetered back and forth. On opening night, he hurried onto the stage to announce: "The fighting has started, Your Majesty. The revolutionists broke through the first line of barricades on the esplanade, and tried to set fire to the city . . ."

As he spoke these words, he jerked his head back, the helmet teetered too far, and fell. Grant caught the helmet in his hands. He tried to save the situation by finishing his line, and did finish it, in a louder voice than usual. Incredible as it may seem, his speech had been edited to end with: ". . . we caught it just in time."

This brought the house down, and it was several minutes before the production could proceed. It was one of several mishaps that occurred to heighten public interest in the plays. Grant's enthusiasm for community drama remained strong, and he devoted much time to it even during intensive painting periods.

While the theater progressed through its early stages, Grant was at work on *Arnold Comes of Age* and *Stone City*. He had done portraits of an elderly man, an elderly woman, and two little girls. Now he wanted to paint a young man.

Arnold Pyle, a young artist about to reach the age of twenty-one, was for five years assistant to Rowan in the Little Gallery. He kept a sharp eye out for prints of paintings by the German or Flemish primitives after Grant became interested in them, and when any came to the gallery he took them to 5 Turner Alley. Pyle was one of a group of artist friends most often at the studio. With Zeman, David McCosh, Marvin and others—Cedar Rapids was full of people who painted—he joined in painting sprees that Grant put on whenever one of Turner's funeral clients asked him to dispose of leftover flowers. The best of the flowers were brought to the studio and Grant and any friends who happened to be there painted them. Flower pictures always sold well.

The portrait of Arnold, like all Grant Wood portraits, told a story. The gauntness of youth was exaggerated, and the eyes were still large and expectant, not yet disillusioned. At the time it appeared, people thought it the best thing Grant had yet done. It won the sweepstakes prize at the 1930 Iowa Art Salon, as the State Fair exhibit is called, and was sold to the Nebraska Art Association at Lincoln.

Stone City took shape in a region far from typical of that part of Iowa. Stone City itself was a ghost town, once a quarrying center, now consisting of a general store and a bridge. It was twenty-six miles northeast of Cedar Rapids and was reached over up-and-down roads. As you topped some of the steep grades, you got the impression that the ground was running away from you into distant depths and that the trees were rising out of it to come floating toward you.

J. A. Green, an Irish pioneer, founded Stone City and brought one thousand workers and steam drills to quarry the limestone that juts out of the ground. Grant could remember as a boy when the steam drills were still in operation, sending jets of steam up over the landscape—it might have made a good painting then too. In 1883, Green was master of all he surveyed, and he built himself a twenty-room stone mansion on the highest hill overlooking the town. He built a stone opera house to bring culture to the town, and a stone church in a less conspicuous place farther down the hill.

In those days limestone was used in railroad abutments as well as in buildings and the quarries did a brisk trade. But with the coming of Portland cement, the business collapsed. By the time Grant came to paint Stone City, no stone had been taken from the place for years. There was plowed ground where the workers had lived in stone huts, and Green's mansion stood hollow and ghostly on top of the hill.

Grant set his easel about fifty yards from the mansion, a corner of which shows at the left of the painting. His arrangement of the ground was somewhat similar to that in sixteenth-century Joachim de Patinir's *Flight into Egypt* in that it sank deep in the foreground and then rose up around, but it was done in racing curves instead of craggy protuberances. As Grant painted them, the hills are fat, the roads loop and glide, the lines seem hurrying to join each other or to get off into the distance. And those bouncing, bowing globular trees seem hardly married to the earth; they look as though they might suddenly rearrange themselves.

On the ground which sloped steeply away from him toward the Wapsipinicon River, he put a cornfield that looks like a brown comforter tied with yellow yarn. In order to stand out, the corn shoots had to be more yellow than green, because the entire painting was done in a greenish tinge which the sixteenth-century landscapes have acquired from age. He left out the church and put in farm buildings, three windmills and some horses and cows—no chickens! A modern bridge over the Wapsie formed the center on which the lines converged, and to the right of the store and water tower he included billboards—the thing he had campaigned against in the *Republican*. He put a Gothic window in a corner of the Green mansion.

Grant said he got the idea for those trees from the bulbous trees on his mother's Haviland china, which she kept "for good" while using ironstone plate for everyday. He may also have been thinking of the lacquered sponges that he set for trees among the models he made for Ely. After the painting appeared, people came to stand where he stood above Stone City. They saw where he got certain ideas, but it didn't look much like the painting. Grant had rearranged as he pleased, to fit his abstract design, which was the starting point for all his pictures.

Stone City was another painting he didn't like when it was finished. "Too damned many pretty curves," he said. "Too many personal mannerisms, caused by fear that because of a close, precise style of painting I might be accused of being photographic. I am having a hell of a time getting rid of these mannerisms."

The public didn't agree with his verdict. Although the impact of *Stone City* and similar stylized landscapes that followed wasn't great at first, their influence was persistent, and their formalized and patterned effect crept into display advertising and landscaping. *Stone City* won the landscape prize at the Iowa Fair in 1930, was sold to the Omaha Society of Liberal Arts, and hung in the Joslyn Memorial Museum. It was the root and stem of the series of bouncing landscapes that came to be associated with the name of Grant Wood.

After each had won prizes in their divisions at the Fair, *Arnold Comes of Age* was chosen over *Stone City* for the sweepstakes award. Probably if the judging had been done later, the decision would have been reversed, though good portraits had a way of appealing to the judges for reasons beyond their technical merits —nothing can be as interesting as a human being.

The incident Grant liked best to tell about *Stone City* occurred while it was on display in the sprawling, high-fenced state fair grounds on the east edge of Des Moines. From a farmer's point of view the landscape had several technical defects: in an area where there was so much flat and rolling land, no farmer would plant corn on a slope as steep as the one Grant showed, nor would he be likely to build barns so close to a river's edge. Grant was interested in getting the comments of farmers on these departures, and saw a farmer examining the painting intently.

"The farmer would get up close to the picture, inspect it and back away, shaking his head," Grant said. "I went up and stood beside him, thinking he would say something about the painting, and sure enough he did. Pretty soon he shook his head more vigorously than ever and said: 'I wouldn't give thirty-five cents an acre for that land.' "

Birth of a Masterpiece

WHEN Grant went back to hard lines and sharp contours, he went
back to Batchelder. Batchelder had laid great emphasis on design;
so did Grant. Batchelder was an admirer of genuine Gothic architecture; so was Grant. Batchelder had been hailed as a man who
was applying European methods to American motifs to produce
distinctively American art; Grant had something of the same nature in mind.

Out of this return to the guidance of his teacher of nearly
twenty years before, out of his new attraction to the Flemish
primitives, his increased preoccupation with small details, and a
new boldness which appeared in his work after the chill reception of his memorial window—out of a combination of all these
things grew *American Gothic.*

The novelty of being an artist and of conforming to standard
practices in order to be accepted had worn off. What he had already achieved seemed worthless. He felt a new kind of freedom.
He took advantage of the fact that he had nothing to lose: first,
to do the kind of work he liked and, second, to strike out for
greater recognition. Instead of mellow, wistful effects, he now
looked for striking qualities and was ready to use strong emphasis
and satire.

He had already made a rough sketch for *American Gothic* when
he saw the house in Eldon. It was done on the back of an envelope,
in a space that could be covered by four postage stamps, and
showed merely a Gothic arch, two long-faced figures and a pitchfork. Even earlier he had shown preoccupation with the Gothic
arch: in 1928 he made a pen-and-ink drawing of his fireplace and

the Gothic-style niche above it—a drawing he later sent in thanks for a decorated scrapbook to G. Alan Chidsey of New York, an admirer whom he never met.

The idea for the design was simply that the lines of a Gothic window showing in the background should be roughly repeated in the faces, and again, upside down, in the tines of the pitchfork. He chose the Eldon house for his background not because he liked it but because he didn't. He thought it a form of borrowed pretentiousness, a structural absurdity, to put a Gothic-style window in such a flimsy frame house. That was to be part of the satire in the painting.

The figures were to be those of a farming couple. Grant looked for models among the farmers, models who would have long faces to fit his design, but couldn't find any. That may have been because he didn't know many farmers and would have had to know them well to be satisfied with their faces.

For the woman, he finally selected his sister Nan, as usual, and for the farmer he picked his dentist, Dr. B. H. McKeeby. Nan knew his plan for the painting—he had told it to half a hundred people—and she wasn't eager to model for it. Grant assured her he would paint her face long and stern, and no one would ever recognize her. He told the same thing to Dr. McKeeby.

The dentist and Grant had been friends for years. Grant had helped decorate his office and home, had brought him a painting of a Paris bridge to pay for a dental bridge, and had undergone long treatments for pyorrhea—Grant's teeth had had no early care. Dr. McKeeby's face had the same fascination for Grant as the old map and the braid on his mother's apron. Once, coming out of a long reverie, he startled Dr. McKeeby by declaring: "I like your face."

Dr. McKeeby, who has not often been accused of being handsome, inquired why.

"Because it's all long straight lines."

Another time Grant seized the dentist's hand. "Let me see your hand." Grant turned the hand over and examined it until Dr. McKeeby wasn't quite sure it was still his own. Finally Grant gave it back, a little apologetically, and said: "You know what that is? That's the hand of a man who can do things."

The hand Grant examined is the hand that holds the pitchfork in *American Gothic*. It looks a little strange there in the painting. Dr. McKeeby holds the pitchfork as though it weren't much bigger than a toothpick, and the thumb seems to protrude farther than is right. But that is a faithful reproduction of the dentist's hand—long, large, big-knuckled with a thumb that is separated to an extraordinary degree from the palm.

To get this remarkable man into the painting became absolutely essential, but when Grant asked him to pose, Dr. McKeeby refused. A modest man, honest and sincere, he said he was a dentist and didn't intend to dip into art. Grant kept after him, and Dr. McKeeby, with good nature, finally agreed—but only on the condition that no one would ever recognize him. It was after the 1929 crash; business was beginning to fall off a little; it didn't require many trips to the studio.

"God knows it can't be beauty you're after," he said.

Grant had him wear a dress shirt, overalls and a dressy coat, to represent a farmer "who might be a preacher on Sundays." Nan, her hair parted in the middle and combed down the sides and her eyes turned aside in self-conscious severity, wore her mother's cameo. Her apron, which Grant picked out of a mail-order catalogue and had sent from Chicago, had the same jagged braid as her mother's. The same snakeplant and the same begonia were placed in the background—on the porch of the house.

Grant intended to satirize the narrow prejudices of the Bible Belt, which includes southern Iowa. He had occasion to deny this later on, but since he was an admirer of H. L. Mencken, Sinclair Lewis and George Bernard Shaw it is easily understood what he had in mind. And he really believed that no one would recognize the models when he got through with them.

Again he painted better than he knew. No one acquainted with Nan or Dr. McKeeby ever failed to recognize them in the painting. Once, Dr. McKeeby sat down in a dining car a thousand miles from home only to have strangers at the table inquire: "Are we by any chance sitting across from one of Grant Wood's characters?"

When *American Gothic* appeared, at the Chicago Art Institute's annual exhibition in 1930, it caused a sensation. Crowds formed in front of it, and people who had never attended an exhibit before heard of it and came down to see it. It was awarded the Harris prize and was bought for the Art Institute for three hundred dollars—the sale price had to be fixed at the time it was entered.

The critics followed with extravagant praise. They called Grant the discovery of the exhibit. They said he was an Iowa Moses who had come to lead art into the Promised Land, and they compared him to Christopher Columbus as a discoverer of America. Grant came as near as an artist can to attaining fame overnight.

Dr. McKeeby felt wretched about the painting. Here he was, one of the best-humored men in the world, a man who really enjoyed life and never wished anybody harm; and there he was, portrayed in all that stark solemnity. Even the prints in the newspapers were good enough to enable his friends to recognize him. He called Grant to his office and, leaning across his desk, pointed a long forefinger at him.

"What did you tell me about that painting?" he demanded in a trembling voice.

Grant was distressed. "Aw, I didn't think anybody would recognize you," he said. Dr. McKeeby never had any doubt that Grant was sincerely sorry and hadn't done it intentionally. Their relations were strained, but Grant kept coming for treatments, and the friendship was never broken.

It would be against Dr. McKeeby's nature to deny anything that was true. He never did deny that it was he who posed for *American Gothic*, but for five years he didn't admit it either. He put questioners off with such remarks as "What do you think?" "Oh, I don't know," or "It could be, I suppose." Sometimes he simply stuck a drill in the questioner's mouth. Finally, in 1935, he admitted that he had posed for it. He wasn't entirely reconciled to the painting, but he wanted to settle the thing once and for all.

Later, when *American Gothic* happened to be in Cedar Rapids, he was asked to pose with Nan for photographs, showing them both beside the painting. Dave Turner put on the pressure. He used persuasion, and Dr. McKeeby liked to be obliging when he could. Dave pointed out that it might never happen again that the dentist, Nan and the painting would all be in Cedar Rapids at the same time.

"I hope some day I can use my face to make such a fellow as Grant Wood a more famous painter," the funeral director declared.

Dr. McKeeby wavered just enough. Then Dave called Mrs. McKeeby and asked her if she had any influence over her husband. Mrs. McKeeby said she did. Dave explained about the photograph, and Mrs. McKeeby promised to have her husband there at the appointed hour. Turner sent a police escort to Dr. McKeeby's office, in an outlying shopping center, and they brought him downtown with sirens going full blast. The photographs were taken.

By this time, Dr. McKeeby's attitude toward the painting had greatly softened. It was suggested to him that there was a good deal of curiosity and wonderment in his expression as it appeared in *American Gothic*. Dr. McKeeby thought that might well be; a dentist, he said, is like anyone else at work and may often be wondering about his children or why he should pass his years in this way. Grant may have absorbed some of that into the painting.

His questioners were encouraged to venture the further opinion that "grim," the adjective usually applied, was the wrong word to describe his expression. It was dry, perhaps, and solemn, and it suggested a firm reliance on a fixed creed, but there was nothing challenging or hostile in it. And there was honesty and character. Now, wasn't Dr. McKeeby himself beginning to like *American Gothic?*

Dr. McKeeby thought a minute and then drew a long breath. "Well sir," he said, "I'd just rather not see it at all."

EIGHTEEN

Version for Iowa

American Gothic, on the actual painting of which Grant spent three months, could have been ready for the Iowa Fair of 1930 but wasn't shown there for obvious reasons. The fair, with its livestock, crop and gardening exhibits and incidental amusement-park features, is primarily for farmers. No one knew what kind of a protest they would raise over being portrayed in this vein.

Grant anticipated trouble, and to mollify the farmers insisted almost from the first that the man in *American Gothic* was a bald-headed, spectacled small-town businessman. There was another good reason for this statement: Dr. McKeeby, who had done inside work all his life, didn't look much like a farmer.

Nan admitted from the beginning that she had posed, and even painted a travesty on *American Gothic*; she put Grant in the middle of it with two tines of the fork sticking up in back of his head for horns, and called it "The Three of Us." A difficulty arose, however, about her place in *American Gothic*: she was obviously so much younger than the sixty-two-year-old Dr. McKeeby that it seemed strange to call them man and wife.

So what had started out to be a farmer and his wife became a small-town businessman and his daughter. Iowa newspapers calling it a farmer and his wife were strongly denounced for their inaccuracy, though that was what it was called outside the state.

But if Dr. McKeeby was a businessman, what was he doing with that pitchfork? His patients often asked that question. "You aren't going to use the pitchfork on me, are you?" they would say as they got into the chair. Dr. McKeeby heard that until, in all good conscience, he thought it just as well there wasn't a pitchfork handy.

The protests from farmers actually were less than Grant expected. Very few farmers said anything at all, though their wives in some cases took up the cudgels in defense of their kind. He received about a hundred letters of protest and a half dozen angry telephone calls when the painting first appeared, and letters continued to trickle in as it became better known.

He issued several statements. He said that there was satire in any realistic picture, that he had tried to characterize truthfully, that to him they were basically good and solid people, and that he hadn't intended to hold them up to ridicule.

What bothered Grant most was a tendency to assume that in *American Gothic* he had simply attempted a composite of what a person would be most likely to see if he drove out into the country. The most frequent and continuing criticism was that the people in the painting weren't typical of Iowa farm folk. Grant finally made it a flat rule that he would not answer any letter that contained the word "typical."

"I never paint anything that is typical," he said angrily, "because if I did I would have to leave out all the interesting detail."

Yet *American Gothic* did suggest a type. The setting and expressions spoke of stubborn lands and rigid, hard-working people; at the same time, the departures from type emphasized the individual reality of these particular subjects—perhaps a type can be effectively represented only by including strong departures from it. And there was never any real doubt that he was thinking of farmers.

The position of the farmers was simple: if Grant was holding them in contempt, of course they weren't going to like it. On the other hand if he was just trying to paint somebody, honestly, as he said—well, artists were funny; maybe it was all right. They heard that Grant painted in overalls. And you had to admit there were people who looked that way. The one with the pitchfork now; he might not be a bad fellow to know.

Grant got along well with farmers, even though later on at his Stone City Art Colony he used nude models and otherwise shocked their sensibilities. The paintings of his Stone City pupils were hung in farmhouses around Cedar Rapids and in fact all over eastern Iowa. And the farmers and the farm wives had nothing to say against him. It was a shame, they said, when the art colony was discontinued. It was a shame when they tore down one of the buildings he had used. He was a fine man.

The Stone City colony, like almost all artists' colonies, operated in the red. Frank Nissen of Cedar Rapids owned the farm on which it was located and came to Grant's studio to collect a two-hundred-dollar rent bill. Grant gave him fifty dollars—to the distress of John Reid, who was trying to settle everything at seventy-five cents on the dollar.

When Reid found out about it, he hurried to 5 Turner Alley. "Don't pay any bills, don't pay any bills, don't give anybody any money"—he thought he had drummed that into Grant's head. Now he was amazed to find that Grant had already paid fifty dollars on the rent, so it was only a hundred and fifty now. Reid climbed the outside wooden stairs and rang the Parisian bell that brought Grant to the door.

"Damn it, didn't I tell you not to pay any bills? Don't you know that I'm sending out letters to all these fellows, asking them to agree to a seventy-five-cent settlement? How can I get them together if you keep dribbling out money?"

"Well, that man was up here and I just happened to have some money so I gave it to him."

"And why in God's name didn't you tell him that I'm handling these Stone City bills?"

"Well, I don't like to say that when I've got the money. It makes me feel uncomfortable."

Reid never did persuade Grant to stop paying bills. It got around that Grant was being bothered a good deal about them. People said it was a shame. Here Cedar Rapids was lucky enough to have an artist who was an artist, and cheap commercial fellows came around pestering him about money, upsetting him, taking his time.

Frank Nissen heard the talk and was conscience stricken. All he was trying to do was collect a bill. He had gone and asked for the money. Grant had given him fifty dollars and had said he would pay the rest later. That was all right. Who would have thought it had anything to do with art?

He never again tried to collect that hundred and fifty dollars or any part of it. The money was still listed as due him when Grant died, and he could have collected it from the estate. But he didn't even want to talk about it.

"Aw, we wrote that off the books," he said. "You shouldn't say that Grant Wood owed money. He was a great artist. We're glad he lived here."

That the people who felt this way about Grant's art constituted a majority there is scarcely any doubt now. Even so, the criticism of *American Gothic* was enough to disturb him. He was sensitive to it, and it probably helped to dissuade him from anything more along the same line. He had had it in mind to paint a circuit-riding minister on horseback, and thought he could do something with a Bible Belt revival meeting. Nothing ever came of these ideas.

So *American Gothic* stood alone. It looked strange hanging there in the Art Institute in Chicago; there was nothing else like it in the room. Not even Grant ever did another painting that had the same odd effect. Its colors were weak, like southern Iowa is during a drought; it got its artistic power from the design; among paintings rich in color, it looked a little like a photograph taken in strong sunlight. It would have been better in a room by itself, a small room with some red plush, gold ornaments and a foot-powered organ to go with the characters. As Grant portrayed them, they did not belong to the well-watered country from which he came but to some poor farming section where people don't have the money to keep up with the times, and turn inward on age-old beliefs.

The personality of the painting was to undergo changes. Some people still saw satire in it, others didn't. Grant started with an idea for satire but painted his subjects with feeling and sympathy —people who saw the painting understood and liked them. Their human characteristics stood out more strongly because of the solemn, arid circumstances in which they were found.

American Gothic has even been classed as heroic. *Fortune* magazine in 1941 wanted to make a war poster of it, with "Government of the people, by the people and for the people" printed underneath. It has become a folkpiece and a symbol, the magazine said, "of the independent spirit which Americans recognize as peculiarly American."

Stone City was also in the 1930 Chicago exhibit, but it won no prize and rated little space in the reviews. At that, it did better than *Woman with Plants* which, at the same exhibit the previous year, failed to raise even one critical eyebrow. It was only after thousands of copies had been distributed among people who knew nothing of technique or form but thought in terms of living that Mrs. Wood's portrait, with its faraway, long-suffering expression and that touch of anxiety to please, began to be highly praised. It struck a chord in the larger public that it had somehow missed at this and other exhibits.

While *American Gothic* was out earning a reputation for him, Grant was back in Cedar Rapids, in his overalls, decorating the

DAUGHTERS OF REVOLUTION

Courtesy of Edward G. Robinson

ARBOR DAY

new Herbert Stamats home. Part of the decoration was an over-mantel painting, an outside view of the house set among balloon-ing and bowing trees.

The plumber looked at the painting and jokingly said: "I put the plumbing in this house, and you haven't given me any credit."

It amused Grant to act on things that came up in light con-versation. He asked how he could give credit for plumbing in an outside view of the house.

They went to the front lawn and looked over the house. The plumber pointed to an outside vent that could show in the paint-ing. Grant roughly sketched its position on a piece of scrap paper. Then he got his brush and put it in.

NINETEEN

Humor in Landscapes

ALTHOUGH *American Gothic* received the acclaim, it was the current of *Stone City* that was running strongest in Grant when the news of his success arrived. He painted *Midnight Ride of Paul Revere*, a good piece of designing by an artist in a good humor.

Midnight Ride of Paul Revere was full of curves and blobs of foliage. It contained what looked to be painting's longest highway, sweeping and curving down to the foreground from the right and then off into the distance on the left. The houses, which had a dollhouse effect, were as modern and well lighted as though a century and a half hadn't passed since Paul Revere kicked up the dust. And the model for the horse was a rocking horse that Grant borrowed from a Cedar Rapids family.

For the Iowa Fair of 1931, he painted *The Appraisal*, a farmer's wife holding an apprehensive hen while a city woman considers it. *The Appraisal* won the sweepstakes in oil at the fair, and Grant turned to *Victorian Survival*, the idea for which he had had for some time. It showed a prim, dried, nineteenth-century woman beside a dial telephone, with a black band around her long straight neck and just enough humor in her face to save the painting from being too stiff.

Herbert Hoover was about to come up for re-election and the house in which he was born stood only thirty-five miles southeast of Cedar Rapids, at West Branch. Grant painted *Birthplace of Herbert Hoover* in fall colors, with flaring trees, a frame house and a concrete highway over which a dark shade was cast by trees full of bananalike curves. In this and other landscapes, he achieved a humorous effect with odd exaggerations which still struck a familiar note.

It was said of *Birthplace of Herbert Hoover* that when it was shown around Iowa it attracted bigger crowds than Hoover himself, which was no great achievement in 1931. When the president saw the painting, he complained that it was too glorified. Only the back half of the house was there when he was born, he said. There was a dirt road in front of it, and the place hadn't looked as well kept as a private golf club.

Grant had rearranged, heightened, stylized and tailored. As one farmer told him, after looking at the painting: "Yep, that's the place all right, and we sure want to thank you for cuttin' them weeds."

With the humorous turn in his work and with his rise from being simply Iowa's first artist to a position as a nationally recognized painter, Grant developed a strong dislike for portrait painting. The reason he gave for his aversion was that people idealized themselves and weren't satisfied to be painted as they actually looked.

"If I paint them the way they really look," he said, "they don't think anything of me. If I paint them the way they want me to, I don't think anything of myself."

Michael Blumberg, a wealthy resident of Clinton, Iowa, came to Cedar Rapids in June of 1931 and asked him to paint a portrait of Melvin Blumberg, Michael's young son. Grant didn't want to do it but wasn't blunt enough to refuse flatly. He went to Dave Turner and asked what he should do.

"Why don't you ask for a lot of money?" suggested Dave. "Ask for five hundred dollars. That ought to slow him up."

Successive stages of the depression were then working their way westward and five hundred sounded like a lot of money. Even some of Grant's prize paintings didn't net him a hundred a month for the time he put in on them, and a hundred and fifty was his standard price for portraits. When he asked for the five hundred dollars, however, Michael Blumberg said, "Fine, I'll take two of them." They settled on eight hundred and fifty for one portrait. The painting of Melvin had to go ahead.

Like his other portraits of the time, Grant's picture of Melvin was forceful and expressive. You got the story at once—a rich man's son who had received plenty of candy and attention and had a new football under his arm. Michael Blumberg was well pleased with it—there was no dissatisfaction on the part of this client—and the portrait of Melvin has taken a place among Grant Wood's major works.

Grant, however, was almost frantic by the time it was completed. He was at the end of an artistic cycle, and this painting was one of the few things he ever did that he didn't want to do. He declared he would paint no more portraits of strangers, and actually did accept only two more portrait commissions during the rest of his life—these more for personal than financial reasons. During the lean years of the depression, he refused at least a dozen portraits that would have brought him around twenty-five hundred dollars each.

As his interest in portraits fell, his new, stylized landscapes matured. He had not lost his old feeling for the lift and sweep of the ground. He painted *Young Corn* and, still in 1931, *Fall Plowing*, and these took their place with *Stone City* and *Birthplace of Herbert Hoover* in a gallery of landscapes that amazed, amused and baffled the country.

Whether Iowa looks as Grant Wood painted it has been debated. Do the trees rise up like huge bunches of toy balloons, or like monstrous, well-trimmed hedgerows, or as solid, overshadowing blobs against the landscape or sky? If you focus your attention on them, no, they don't: they look like trees anywhere else. But if you are barely conscious of them, not seeing too closely, they do create these impressions. And the ground does seem to bend and glide and roll off into the distance. Grant's painting, called unreal realism, had a realistic effect; something basic and instantly recognizable in the landscape had been selected and emphasized, and Iowans who had left the state were reminded powerfully of home.

As Whistler said, "Seldom has nature succeeded in creating a picture." Grant didn't expect to find one ready made. He explained his weird shapes as a compromise between design and reality. "All my pictures are first planned as abstractions," he said. "I make a design of abstract shapes without any naturalistic details. Until I am satisfied with this abstract picture, I don't go ahead. When I think it's a sound design, then I start very cautiously making it look like nature. But I'm so afraid of being photographic that maybe I stop too soon."

To illustrate the importance of repetition in design, he once displayed a photograph beside a drawing he had made of corn ears hung against a barn to dry for seed. In his drawing, the ears were all the same size and they moved in a regular, animated procession in line with the gabled roof. In the photograph, they were odd-sized, and they straggled and sagged lifelessly. At dusk when shapes and lines are indistinct, they might momentarily give the effect he produced, but in the hard light of day they offered nothing of interest until he reorganized them.

Young Corn was hung in Woodrow Wilson High School in Cedar Rapids. *Fall Plowing* won the landscape prize at the 1932 Iowa Fair—Grant's last fair prize—and was bought for the collection of Marshall Field III. Gardner Cowles, Jr., of Des Moines bought *Birthplace of Herbert Hoover*, and Mrs. C. M. Gooch of Memphis got *Midnight Ride of Paul Revere*. Against the tide of the depression, Grant's fame continued to spread.

His rise was still based chiefly, however, on *American Gothic*. The picture grew in popular esteem in a way that could not have been foreseen. In 1930, it was apparent only that it had received unusual praise and had won a three-hundred-dollar prize, in an exhibit where the prizes ran up to twenty-five hundred dollars. Most of these prize paintings were comfortably forgotten within a year, and their names lived on only in small type after the artist's name in Who's Who, or in obituaries prepared for publication on the artist's death.

But *American Gothic* in 1931 was taken to London, where it created another sensation. More than this, its fame spread among people not otherwise interested in art. Its title alone had sound and rhythm and romantic appeal, like the Cardiff Giant, the Cherry Sisters (also Cedar Rapids products), and the Great Stone Face. *American Gothic* rolled on the tongues even of people who were scarcely sure it was a painting. There was an awesome quality about it, too. It was as though four centuries had been rolled back and a genuine old master, like those mentioned with such deference in the history books, had been found mysteriously alive, painting in Iowa. And to it was added the interest stirred up by dramatized accounts of the controversy it had created: Iowa farmers were supposed to be up in arms. People wanted to see what could have caused such a row.

Grant's celebrity reached the point where his landscapes, however good, could scarcely live up to his reputation. He needed something that would reach far beyond the limits of purely artistic appreciation; something that would reach the ordinary person. And he found it in social issues. Popular interest had turned to politics. With the deepening of the depression, people who had taken no notice of elections before, and in fact had had nothing to gain or lose by them, rose against reaction.

All his life Grant had been a Democrat, and it was something to be a Democrat in Cedar Rapids, one of the most Republican places in the country. The only thing he had had to gloat over was the re-election of Woodrow Wilson, and that greatly pleased him

HUMOR IN LANDSCAPES

—Paul Hanson and Ralph Conybeare had had a good time making fun of him and his candidate. Grant was so isolated politically that he had grown accustomed to keeping silent on the subject—so much so that many of his friends thought he wasn't interested in politics.

Among those of like thinking, however, he talked freely. He thought in terms of people, not entries in ledger books, and believed in big government projects to raise the level and quality of living. He didn't think it right that the great majority should have to work so hard, while the few enjoyed luxuries and good living. As Hazel Brown put it: "He was a New Dealer before there was a New Deal."

His isolation was coming to an end, for now the views he favored were beginning to spread. The time was ripe to strike a blow. And besides being a blow for the things he believed in, it would strike against those stiff-necked, vitriolic supernationalists who had denounced his Memorial Window because it was made in Germany. He reached for the sharpest weapon in painting—satire. He painted *Daughters of Revolution.*

TWENTY

"Those Tory Gals"

Daughters of Revolution took shape in 1932. Ostensibly Grant used no models for it, though there are people in Cedar Rapids who will offer to tell you the names of those three tight-lipped ladies who appear in the painting. The only part of the picture anybody will claim is the hand holding the teacup.

That is Miss Prescott's hand. Grant called her up in the middle of one afternoon, and in his usual bland, measured speech asked:

"Could you come over?"

"Well, after all, I do have a job here."

"Aw, you don't do anything there; come on over."

So Miss Prescott went to 5 Turner Alley and primly held a teacup while Grant sketched her hand. It might be considered part of her work, she thought; after all, Grant had done a lot for the school. Besides she was glad, as she put it, to have a hand in the picture. Grant kept saying, "I can't get this hand, I can't get this hand"—he had tried several other models without getting a hand to suit him.

It had to be a very special hand, one that would appear to be hooked onto a ledge of prestige, besides holding a teacup. The whole idea of the picture was to show three smug, tea-sipping ladies in all their stiff pride of birth in front of Emanuel Leutze's painting, *Washington Crossing the Delaware*, with its dashing figures of the revolutionists from whom such ladies claim descent. Grant at first called it "Daughters of American Revolution," but Ely had visions of a real tornado of protest and persuaded him to take the word "American" out.

Grant took care that a member of the D.A.R. should see the

painting in an incomplete stage, and her public denunciation laid the groundwork for its forthcoming publicity. The first photographs of it were released in September, 1932, amid laughter from the public and anguished outcries from the D.A.R. and its friends.

By the time it reached the Carnegie International Exhibition in Pittsburgh for its first appearance, *Daughters of Revolution* was the center of such a controversy that the exhibitors weren't sure they ought to show it. They compromised by placing it carefully behind a door casing, hoping to attract as little attention as possible.

Their hopes were not realized. It almost seemed as though there were no other painting in the exhibit. The Sons of the American Revolution demanded that it be withdrawn from public display. The D.A.R. took no action as an organization, but the comments of its members seemed to come right out of the painting.

"The D.A.R. will carry on its work regardless of these human gnats that buzz around us"—the words seemed to come from the solid, complacent woman on the left. "Most such attacks begin with the Reds"—that might have come from the fierce, frozen lady with the teacup. "Why should an organization with such a laudable purpose as the D.A.R. be held up to ridicule?"— and that from the fuddled, starry-eyed woman on the right.

The critics generally took Grant's side. One wrote: "This picture will create a great deal of talk and a great deal of hard feelings—but not enough." The author and lecturer Louis Untermeyer declared: "That picture—*Daughters of Revolution*—is a complete Sinclair Lewis novel. Why the very words 'communism' or 'revolution' make the D.A.R.'s froth at the mouth. And there they are, praising Washington—Washington, the revolutionist."

Grant called it "a pretty rotten painting, carried by its subject matter"—a piece of irony; the D.A.R.'s weren't complaining about his technique. More seriously, he said: "I don't like toryism; I don't like people who are trying to set up an aristocracy of birth in a Republic." He referred to the painting as "Those Tory Gals."

He had been particularly offended because Jane Addams, whom he greatly admired, was placed on a D.A.R. undesirable list. He didn't like the idea of an undesirable list, which he thought was used to club people, especially less fortunate people, over the head.

"They could ladle it out," he said. "I thought I'd see if they could take it. Besides," he added, "I'd rather have people rant and rave against my painting than to pass it up with 'Isn't that a pretty picture?' " He was satisfied that he had struck a "real blow." He had done what an artist could toward the election of Roosevelt, and had helped create atmosphere for the beginning of the New Deal.

He drew a portrait of himself at this time, and it won first prize at the annual exhibit of the Iowa Federation of Women's Clubs in November, 1932. The self-portrait was in an almost heroic mood. The straps of his overalls were looped over the collar of a sports shirt open at the neck, and corn shocks, globular trees and windmill familiar to his paintings showed in the background. It was Grant Wood, the farmers' painter, as he lived in Cedar Rapids and as he liked to be known.

Daughters of Revolution was on display alongside *American Gothic* and *Midnight Ride of Paul Revere* at Chicago's Century of Progress with its sixty million paid admissions. Postcard reproductions of the paintings exhibited were sold at a nearby booth. Some of the world's great masterpieces were hung in the hall, but Grant Wood's pictures were what the public wanted.

"We sell more *Daughters of Revolution* than anything else," one of the counter girls confided. "Even members of the D.A.R. buy it; I know because they're wearing the pins. Sometimes it's their husbands that buy it; they say they're tired of hearing about the family tree. *American Gothic* is popular too. And we sell a lot of this *Paul Revere's Ride*."

Through the bold early years of the New Deal, *Daughters of Revolution* continued to grow in popularity because of the long story it told—from the landings of the pioneers and the struggles to overthrow the titles and some of the privileges of birth, to these tea-sipping ladies, trying to introduce hardening of the arteries in an otherwise still-young country. Except for recognition of these narrative qualities, the artistic rating given it wasn't high.

The painting was sold to Edward G. Robinson, who said it amused him. Some of the anger it stirred up was more real than humorous. Grant thought that his pioneer ancestry and his membership in the American Legion were all that saved him from being physically attacked. Most of the anger, however, was laughed off. Even when the picture was flashed on a screen at an Iowa D.A.R. convention it provoked laughter. Miss Prescott once came upon a group of women standing in front of the painting, denouncing it.

"Why it's ridiculous," she heard one of the women say. "Look at that hand. Nobody has a hand like that."

Miss Prescott struck a pose. She held up her hand in that prim way she had held the teacup.

"Ladies," she said, "I overheard one of you say that nobody has a hand like that. I want you to see such a hand. In fact this is exactly the hand you see in the painting."

Arbor Day, nostalgic for the past, progressed side by side with the two-fisted *Daughters of Revolution*. Grant was used to painting for a purpose, and the purposes of the two pictures were entirely different. *Daughters of Revolution* was a venture into rough-and-tumble politics, *Arbor Day* a memorial to two teachers, Catherine Motejl and Rose Waterstradt.

Miss Prescott suggested the idea for *Arbor Day*. She had been driving in the country one day with Miss Motejl and they had stopped at a country schoolhouse where Miss Motejl had once taught. Miss Prescott commented on the fine grove of trees around it. Miss Motejl said: "Yes, we planted them all ourselves."

There was something in that remark that touched Miss Prescott. She thought of all the years this good lady had worked with children to plant and look after those trees. Now the children were gone, and the trees had grown up to dwarf the squat schoolhouse. And Miss Motejl, sitting there in the car, old and dried up, with not much longer to look at them, was saying weakly: "Yes, we planted them all ourselves."

After Miss Motejl and Miss Waterstradt had died and the matter of the memorial had come up, Miss Prescott thought of that afternoon and suggested to Grant that he paint something about a country school, something about tree planting. The sun was shining and it was fine weather when she made the suggestion. Grant put the idea in the back of his head, and by the time he got to it, it was bitter cold, below zero. He called Miss Prescott on the telephone.

"Would you like to go out and look at schoolhouses today?"

"Oh yes, sure. It's a fine day for it, isn't it?"

Grant persuaded her to go, though it was so cold she scarcely thought her car would start. They managed to get under way, and looked at several country schools, but none of them would do. Grant had a quart of whisky along, and at each school took a drink. With the need for fortifying himself against the cold and with the delay in finding a proper school, the process went on until Grant, as Miss Prescott described it, was higher than a cat's back. By the time they found the right schoolhouse, he was in a mellow mood.

"Why don't I paint a picture of all the things that are passing —the one-room school, the belfry, the horse and wagon, the pump, the coal shed, the outhouse, the walking plow, the dirt road?"

And they are the things that went into *Arbor Day*, along with the original idea—a schoolhouse and a teacher directing an oddly assorted group of children in the planting of a tree. This was the kind of scene in which Miss Motejl, nearly fifty years before, had started her grove of trees—a farmer driving past in a grain wagon, another walking behind a plow, a boy at the pump for water, a dirt road snaking into the distance between piecrust-edged road-banks. Immense billowing reaches to treeless land stretched in every direction from the schoolhouse; Grant seemed to get more ground into a small painting than anybody else alive. This was one of his best pictures.

The depression continued. Though Grant was painting stead-ily, his income was small. "You are the unluckiest sucker that ever lived," John Reid used to tell him. "Right when you become fa-mous, everybody loses all their money." Grant complained about this, too. "Now that I could get some money for my paintings, nobody's got any money to buy them," he would say—though he wasn't enough interested in money to paint meaningless portraits. He finally went to Miss Prescott and suggested, in a tentative and uncertain way, that he "could make some money" by selling *Arbor Day* elsewhere.

The painting had already been hung in McKinley High School. It was a memorial to two teachers, whom both Miss Prescott and Grant had known well. A good many objections could have been made. But Miss Prescott had her own ideas about right and wrong —especially when it came to pictures. Grant needed money. She let him take it.

Grant sold *Arbor Day* for twelve hundred dollars. He wanted to refund the two hundred he had been paid by the school for painting it, but Miss Prescott said no, he should paint another picture and replace it, and that would make it all right. He painted *Tree Planting*, which was hung in the memorial place at the school. He later used his sketch for *Tree Planting* for one of his first lithographs.

Still in 1932, Grant painted *Fruits of Iowa,* a series of five mural hangings for the Montrose Hotel in Cedar Rapids. Here he was interested only in line. He borrowed Hazel and Mary's cleaning woman for one of the pictures because she was "all in round curves." The pictures were filled with round-shouldered men and women, round geese, round pigs, round corn, beans and watermelons. The major part of one of the paintings was taken up by the rear end of a cow. It amused Grant to make the cow's tail as straight and stiff as a poker. To those who were interested in line, these were very good murals; to others they seemed to lack human characterization and to have something in common with the cow's tail—stiff, not a good example of his work.

Arbor Day was entered in the 1932 Iowa Fair, but *Fall Plowing* took the big prize. It was the fourth straight year that Grant had won the sweepstakes in oil. He then permanently retired from state fair competition. He was like a heavyweight champion retiring undefeated, to give the others a chance—an action that was praised in the newspapers and that caused some gnashing of teeth among painters who held their artistic achievements well above his. His next landscape, *Near Sundown,* which was sold to Katherine Hepburn, was more naturalistic than those that grew out of *Stone City,* and he followed it with *Spring Landscape* and *Autumn Oaks,* which were still more naturalistic. The period of bounding and bouncing landscapes, like the period of portrait painting, was over.

TWENTY-ONE

Stone City Colony

FOR some reason the limestone that lies in tilted beds under Iowa's soil came to the surface around Stone City. It pushed up the ground in a series of hills and ridges. The Wapsipinicon has cut a deep valley through them, and it ducks under trees that grow out of the steep banks and almost meet overhead. There is relief in this stony section, after so much rolling land all around. It is a place for ghosts to hide out, for small boys to explore caves under limestone ledges and for artists to find how feverish the usually complacent lines of the Iowa landscape can become.

The pioneer J. A. Green liked it there. When he built his stone mansion and looked out over the steam drills and the hard-working men who were cutting blocks of limestone from just under the topsoil, he saw a great future for these hills. Then Portland cement came, and Green and his workers went away. The smaller stone houses fell down, and the ghosts and the Wapsipinicon resumed their meditations.

In 1932, intruders came again. It wasn't at first apparent what they were after. They stood on the tops of the hills and gestured with their arms. They poked around the mansion and the opera house and the circular water tower and the warehouse that Green had left behind. Most puzzling of all, they brought out a caravan of ten old ice wagons, tied in a row behind a truck.

The ice wagons were ranged along the brow of Green's hill, like circus wagons ready to leave. Perhaps they were going to keep animals up there. No, not animals, the word went around; not animals, but artists. Artists were going to live in those ice wagons. Artists were going to live in the mansion, and in the water tower, and anywhere else they might decide to bed down. The whole hill would be covered with artists. It would be called the Stone City Art Colony.

Grant took time out while working on *Daughters of Revolution* to found the colony. It was to offer a six weeks' summer course, for which college credit could be arranged through Coe College. The rates were fixed: $40 tuition for the full six weeks, $7.50 by the week, $4 an hour for private instruction; $6 for six weeks' space in the men's dormitory, $1.50 by the week, fifty cents a week for camping space, $8.50 a week for board. "Excellent cuisine" was guaranteed; no linen, towels or blankets would be furnished. There was a sort of double-or-nothing arrangement with the printer for the first pamphlet announcements: if the colony was a success, he could add something to his bill; if not, he would forget about it.

The idea for the ice wagons came from James Kelley, a Davenport artist, and he got it from watching gypsies in Mexico.

"There's nothing better to live in than a wagon," Kelley said. "It won't blow over in a windstorm, and it has a dry, raised floor in case of wet weather."

Grace Boston was appointed business manager for the colony. She found ten old wagons belonging to the Hubbard Ice Company. The wagons had begun to droop, standing month after month in all kinds of weather with their tongues out, waiting for horses that never came—the company wasn't using horses any more. Miss Boston approached the owner, Joseph T. Chadima, and asked for them.

"We want them for artists' bunks," she told him. "We want to use them instead of tents at the Stone City Art Colony."

"Art?" said Chadima. "Well, I guess it is important, even in these times, since so many people are talking about it."

Unfortunately, Miss Boston admitted, they couldn't offer him any money, but if he would give them the wagons they would present a scholarship, a full six weeks' scholarship, to whomever he selected. Chadima (whose name is entirely plausible in Cedar Rapids, where a large part of the population is Czech) said he'd think it over.

"You know, I like that idea," he told her later. Miss Boston said fine, whom did he want to give the scholarship to? Well, he didn't have anybody in mind, he just liked the idea. Couldn't he suggest someone who ought to have it? No, no, she could give it to anybody she pleased.

So the deal was closed. The scholarship was given to Julia Sampson, who had been the most promising art student in Grant High School and who couldn't go to the colony that summer without a scholarship because her parents wanted her to finish a business course instead. Interesting things like this got into the newspaper in Cedar Rapids.

A special permit had to be obtained from the State Highway Commission at Ames to transport the ten sagging wagons the twenty-six miles to Stone City. The permit was issued, and preparations went ahead. The third floor of Green's mansion was set up as a men's dormitory, and women were given space on the second floor; classrooms, kitchen, dining room, and recreation room filled up the house. A lithographing and picture-framing shop was set up in the basement.

Grant's title was "faculty director." He took one of the ice wagons for himself and painted a mural on the outside of it—a craggy scene with a buck deer poised on one pillar of stone and an Indian brave on another, and snow-capped mountains in the background. This precedent was followed by every holder of an ice wagon; in some cases the painting of gaudy or heroic scenes on a decrepit wagon took most of the six weeks' course.

The teaching talent included Edward Rowan, Adrian Dornbush, who had come to Cedar Rapids the previous winter from Flint, Michigan, to teach in the Little Gallery, Grant, Marvin,

Arnold Pyle, Leon Zeman, and David McCosh, all of Cedar Rapids, and Florence Sprague, a Des Moines sculptor. Courses were offered in life drawing, outdoor painting from life, color theory, sketching in oil, sketching in water color, composition, lithographing, metalcraft, picture framing and sculpture.

"It should be clearly understood that we are not trying to promote our own particular methods of painting," wrote Grant in the announcement, "our theory being that when a painter has a definite message he will, by experiment, find the most adequate means of expressing it, let the result be as conservative, as eclectic or as radical as it may."

The response was gratifying. One hundred and twenty students attended during the first summer, and there were usually fifty or more on the ten-acre grounds at one time. Grant, as usual, wore overalls, and so did some of the others. Shorts, khaki trousers, an occasional beret, and an occasional smock made their appearance. It was a very motley assemblage.

A breakfast bell rang at 7:30 A. M., and those who liked could put in a full day, although attendance at most of the classes wasn't compulsory. Meals were served in "dinner for threshers" style. The mortality on dishes was high in the kitchen, where they were tossed about by amateur jugglers. Half the students were either on scholarships or were working their way, which proved an obstacle to balancing the colony's books.

The opera house to which Green had hoped to bring vocal talent was given over to exhibitions of paintings. The feudal halls from which he had expected to administer his small empire of stone were decorated with such pictures as Byron Boyd's painting of Lenin's tomb, done in Moscow two years before. Instead of fine wines and liquors in the cellar, beer was served over a rough-board counter in what was known as "The Sickle and Sheaf." The earthen floor was left bare; a wagon wheel hung from the ceiling as a light fixture; mugs, flagons and goblets sat against the wall, and in one corner was a painting of a villainous traveling salesman with a Jack Diamond mustache and a coy and buxom farmer's daughter.

Indoor instruction proved unpopular, and a good part of the teaching was done on excursions up the valley and to surrounding farms. Care had to be taken not to drop any palette scrapings on the grass; cattle might eat them and be poisoned. Chickens, thinking them worms, sometimes crept up to peck at the long ribbons of alizarin that the artists squeezed from their tubes—a practice that had to be vigorously discouraged to avoid offending the farmers.

Nude models proved a problem. Once properly undraped and posed, they were defenseless against flies and other insects, and squirmed and flinched to the despair of the artists. The problem was solved for all time when someone thought of spraying them with antifly fluid. Models could be obtained in the surrounding country—one girl's mother came with her the first day, but after she was satisfied that the artists were more interested in their work than in looking at her undressed daughter she let the girl come alone.

Soon after the artists arrived and settled themselves, visitors began turning off the concrete highway three miles away and driving along rutted roads and up steep hills to see what was going on. Open house was held on Sundays, and ten cents admission was charged. The band from the Men's Reformatory at Anamosa furnished music; hot dogs and pop were sold; paintings were exhibited and offered for sale. As many as a thousand persons on a single Sunday afternoon walked up the steep grade to see what an artists' colony was like and to look at the paintings.

"We have a price tag on every picture," Grant said. "Roughly a picture thirteen inches by fifteen would cost about fifteen dollars."

This statement was for publication, and there was an artist's optimism in it. Any visitor who couldn't get a thirteen-by-fifteen painting for less than fifteen dollars wasn't much of a buyer. Some of them sold for twenty-five cents, and any amount between five and ten dollars was a good price. The depression was at its depth.

Adrian Dornbush took over the loft of the circular water tower which was above a deep well, and this became known as "Adrian's Tomb." The loft was reached by an outside ladder that sometimes mysteriously disappeared while he was up there. He was given to pets, and by the second year needed a house. He rented one in a nearby valley and lived there with his mother, his dog Rex, his cat Herbie, and his rooster Franklin.

One woman who was writing a novel enrolled and paid her tuition, but she didn't want any instruction in art. She didn't want to be bothered, either; she wanted to finish her novel. Some came to study the place, to find how the thing was run, or to talk to Grant. Among the distinguished visitors was John Steuart Curry; he and Grant met for the first time there. They were curiously alike, both short and stocky, both deliberate, both given to farm painting.

What must have puzzled the ghosts of Stone City most was a morose mule that wandered about among the easels and looked balefully at the artists and their work. This sad-eyed animal was brought back from New Orleans by Dave Turner. He and a companion had wandered into an auction there and, moved by the spirit of the bidding, bought the mule for $32.50 and paid the freight on it to Cedar Rapids.

Dave kept the mule in his garage for a while. One day it kicked him. Dave kicked back. His wife Hilda, not having seen the mule let loose, called him down for cruelty to a dumb animal. Dave thought he had had enough of this mule and all the trouble it could cause. He got Grant on the telephone at the Stone City colony.

"I'm sending you a present," he began.

"It's not that mule, is it?"

"Yes, it is."

"No, not that. I won't have it. We've got no place for it. This is an art colony. We . . ."

"Too late, it's on its way," Dave broke in, and hung up the receiver.

The mule arrived at Stone City, but the fine artistic atmosphere of the colony failed to interest it, and despite every care it died there, sorrowing for the south.

TWENTY-TWO

Art Comes to the Farm

IT WAS difficult to prevent the cultural efforts of the Stone City colony from taking a humorous turn. On one occasion Grant went over to lend his prestige to the art competition at a nearby county fair. He didn't take part in the judging, which would have involved several hours of sorting through earnest offerings; he was scheduled to make the awards.

When he got there, he found that the first prize for still life had been assigned to a picture of a baby. He looked up the fair manager. Technical difficulties had arisen, he explained; "still life" didn't mean exactly what the words implied. The manager got the point, but didn't see how they could make a change: they had already announced the winner; to change with such an explanation would be very embarrassing.

"Let's go ahead with it," said the manager. "After all, the baby's still alive, isn't it?"

Grant made the presentation.

Among the thousands of visitors who came to the colony on Sundays were elderly ladies who wanted to ask Grant a question: was it true that the three tines of the pitchfork in *American Gothic* symbolized the Blessed Trinity? He told them no, it was a nice idea, perhaps, but the fact was that the pitchfork symbolized only a pitchfork.

The legend persisted. It seemed to travel in a channel of its own, beyond the reach of denials. It had been started in one of the nationally distributed religious papers, where a critic profoundly asserted it to be a fact. This led to the formation of "The Banana Oil Art Research Society to Razz and Befuddle Fancy Art Critics," and a series of "Whereas," "Whereas," and

"Whereas" petitions were drawn up, supposedly for presentation to such critics.

With all the fooling, however, the colony was primarily a place of hard work. Few students stayed in bed after the breakfast bell, and the days were spent in long hikes and in a fever of sketching and painting. Young artists felt that this was the "real thing." They were there in the open, studying under an artist who had made contact with the public and thus given significance to his work.

"Art isn't worth a damn if you can't make these people around here appreciate it," Grant told them. "An art that loses contact with the public is lost," he used to say, and on other occasions: "Art for art's sake is dead," and "We must get back to simple relations between the artist and the public."

There were artists who seemed to consider it a disadvantage if their work appealed to the public. They would rather produce something only they themselves, if even they, could understand. To Grant, this meant that art would have to exist as a biteless, tolerated parasite on the wealthy and intellectual few, while a small group of artists preened themselves on being a people apart. Strong measures were taken to discourage this kind of Bohemianism. When a group called the Greenwich Village clique gradually formed within the colony, Adrian Dornbush was assigned the job of breaking it up. He delivered a lecture before the assembled students on what would be permitted and what wouldn't.

"If you don't want to paint under these auspices, get out," he wound up, and walked with flushed face from the room.

Although Grant emphasized that he wasn't promoting any particular method and frequently said "Don't paint like me; don't copy anybody," he actually taught his own basic methods. The difference between his method and some other usually seemed to him the difference between right and wrong.

He used a fifty-fifty mixture of linseed oil and turpentine, and didn't like to have the proportions changed. He preferred panel boards to canvas—most of his paintings were on panel—and pressboard was what was used, for the most part, at Stone City. Some of the students earned their tuition putting on the original coat of eggshell-white paint which served as a base on these panels.

Grant insisted that the students make a pencil sketch, even if it was only on an envelope. He also insisted that a rough outline of the sketch be put on the board with charcoal before any painting began—the charcoal to be rubbed off later. He disliked vague titles like "Nocturne" and "Flowers in Spring"; if you couldn't get a specific title, you didn't have an idea. He advised examining pictures upside down as well as right side up; if they weren't still in balance when they were upside down, there was something wrong.

He delivered no formal lectures. He wandered from easel to easel. He didn't hesitate to reach over a student's shoulder and paint in something that was needed. He usually made some comment, good or bad, on anything he looked at. Sometimes he translated his comment into action.

Sturges Ely, Henry S. Ely's son, was a student at Stone City. Once Grant looked distastefully at something Sturges had done and asked: "Sturg, have you got a palette knife?" Sturges handed him the knife. With three downward strokes, Grant cut through the paint and undid Sturges' work. Then he handed the knife back and walked on.

A picture should never say "Aren't I pretty"; it should say "Here I am," and it should say more than that. If it didn't convey an idea, Grant said, it wasn't a medium of expression, and he strongly felt that it should get its idea across to the average, factual-minded person.

He admitted that at one time or another he had been guilty of everything he denounced. That painting of the piece of music, now—ugh. And some of those things he had done in Europe—ugh. Because of this kind of talk, because of his mild manner, and because of his prestige among younger artists, he was able to enforce his ideas without offending people.

There was no separation of teachers and students. They ate at the same long tables, and in the evenings sat together on Green's lawn overlooking the solitary remains of Stone City, the store building and the bridge, the hills gashed with abandoned stone quarries, and the woods of oak, hickory and elm. Because of the height of Green's hill, it was cool there, and mosquitoes seldom bothered them.

Grant was forty-one years old during the first session of the colony and forty-two during its second and last summer. His weight was close to 185 pounds, but in his overalls he didn't look fat; he looked muscular, ruddy and broad-browed. He had changed from horn-rimmed spectacles to thin-rimmed glasses. His hair had receded somewhat in front and a bald spot was forming on the back of his head.

"There's a great future for you fellows here in the midwest," he would say. "It's new, it isn't already covered with palette scrapings." He told how, when he was painting in Europe, he would often find palette scrapings on the ground where he was standing or would see where other artists had wiped their brushes on a nearby fence. "Why should I have painted what a hundred artists had painted before?" he would ask. "I might as well have been sending home postcards."

Grant sometimes got his classes up as early as 2:00 A. M. to go painting at sunrise. More often they went in the afternoon. There was never any doubt about where they were going; Grant always knew "a good place to paint." He had that kind of definiteness about anything connected with art.

Besides, this was Stone City, the Wapsipinicon valley, where he had explored and counted birds as a boy and where he had painted his first great landscape and many that went before. He had been over most of the ground on foot. And this colony was the nearest he ever came to the thing he had had in mind when he imagined a whole row of studios along Turner Alley. His ideas were different then, but they came from the same basic urge—to have a school of his own.

"I don't think I'm any great shakes as a painter," he told John Reid, "but I do hope to influence this younger generation and the people of the midwest toward the art of the midwest."

Did the farmers cuss these artist fellows who were painting naked women up on the hill? Well, to tell the truth, they didn't; they felt more or less included in the project. When a class wanted to go on a farm, Grant went up to the farmhouse and asked permission, and without exception he was told they could go wherever and paint whatever they pleased. He was likely to come back with a sackful of something to eat.

Often there were half a dozen or more students with their easels set at different angles around a barn. The cows tossed their heads and shied away, but the farmers steered them through the gates and the painting went on. If certain members weren't through when it was time to go back for dinner, the rest of the class went on, and the stragglers ate in the kitchen.

The crowds visiting the colony on Sundays became so great that some of the all-too-many students who were working their way were engaged in parking automobiles on the grounds. Paintings competed with hamburger sandwiches and soft drinks for the market, and often didn't bring much more. It wasn't a good idea to sell nudes; you could try the farmers too far on this point. Most of the pictures sold were landscapes, farm scenes or model studies, though there was complete freedom as to subject matter so long as it was understandable. Dennis Burlingame, who had been with a circus for seven years, spent his time at the colony painting clowns and other circus subjects.

The students were encouraged to sell their work for whatever they could get. High asking prices were discouraged. Grant even suggested attaching written explanations to help sell them, though for himself and established artists he disliked catalogue explanations. The paintings were displayed with price tags on them all during Sundays, and toward evening an auction was held for what was left over.

Ordinarily the students kept whatever their pictures brought, but at the end of the term an auction was held for the benefit of the colony. Grant contributed paintings for the occasion, as did the others. At a considerable wrench to his feelings, Sturges Ely contributed the best thing he had done.

It was a really good painting, of an unusual octagonal farmhouse, and it had the kind of specific title Grant liked: "R.F.D. 121." Sturges looked at it a long time before he gave it up, but his school spirit was strong, he felt that this had been a high point of his life, and he wanted to do all he could to help out.

When "R.F.D. 121" came up for auction, the first offer was twenty-five cents. The bidding was spirited, and the price rose and rose—fifty—sixty—seventy. It was finally knocked down to the highest bidder for seventy-five cents.

TWENTY-THREE

Woman with Chicken

GRANT had a strong feeling that the impressions of childhood and youth were deeper and more lasting than any that came later. When he wanted to sum up what happened during his change from the restful to the forceful, he said: "I went back to my boyhood and the impressionable years for material, and that is what happened to American painting."

He spoke with contempt of "self-conscious technical exercises, peeled off the top layer of experience." He didn't think you could paint a picture unless it was based on something you had felt for a long time, something rooted back in earlier years. It took that long for feeling to develop in him.

"Technique does not constitute art," he said. "Nor is it a vague, fuzzy romantic quality known as 'beauty,' remote from the realities of everyday life. It is the depth and intensity of an artist's experience that are the first importance in art."

Next to his mother, the person he knew best was his sister Nan. Ever since she had begun to walk, he had been determined that she should be an artist, and had disputed for years on the point with Aunt Sarah Wood, who insisted that "one artist in the family is enough." (Aunt Sarah won a temporary victory when she paid Nan's tuition at a Cedar Rapids business college, for which reason Nan felt obliged to attend for two years, but after less than a year of office work she went back to painting.)

Nan was at home a good deal during the early thirties. Her husband had been ill for some time and had to have hospital care, so she came to 5 Turner Alley. Grant decided to paint her portrait. She was to wear a polka-dot blouse in the picture, and they couldn't find one with large enough dots. Grant looked around the kitchen and saw what he wanted—a biscuit cutter. With it he cut round slices from a potato, inked them and stamped the dots on a white blouse. Then he got a young chicken to place in her hand, and went ahead with the painting.

He worked sixteen weeks on *Portrait of Nan*. Here was a subject far better than some stranger who might stop at his studio. He placed the emphasis on the long straight nose and gave her a solemn downward expression. It was somewhat more stylized than his 1929 portraits, but it had a quality in common with them—the feeling of the artist for the subject, and a sense of the subject's character.

Grant was the kind who took offense, suffered over trivialities and became mired in controversies. Nan wasn't. No feud was so fierce that she couldn't get along with both sides. To her, he was the artist; although she did considerable painting herself she always disparaged her ability and didn't set her opinions against his. She had a calming effect on him.

There is that feeling in the portrait, of an absorbing steadiness. It was an addition to his gallery of portraits that seemed to belong to another century—to a time when moods were less changeable, when time wasn't a luxury and the currents of life ran more slowly and at greater depth.

Grant liked *Portrait of Nan*. It was the only one of his major works that he kept for himself, and it hung on his wall until he died. He liked the chicken she held in her hand, too, and kept it at the studio after he was through with the painting. Perhaps an apartment-studio isn't the place for a live chicken, but there it was. It ate heartily in its box, and grew to adolescence. Then a tragedy occurred.

No. 5 Turner Alley was still a center for amateur theatricals. Mrs. Wood's housekeeping was often upset as props were dragged in for a showing to be given in front of one of the dormer windows while the audience, if any, sat in the other. Grant helped coach one community drama group to a state championship, won at the University of Iowa in 1932. Among the accoutrements of the players was a rubber cigarette that was left lying about the studio.

The chicken is not to be blamed for what happened. It was only an adolescent chicken, and it had not been out in the world. It escaped from its box to stretch its legs about the studio, saw that rubber cigarette, thought it was a worm, and gobbled it down. The cigarette stuck in the poor fowl's gullet, and it died a slow death of strangulation.

No gain seemed likely to offset this loss to the Wood household, but when the chicken was picked and the pinfeathers were still on it and the rubber cigarette was still in its neck, Grant had an idea. A little straightening out and unifying of those pinfeathers, some more length in that neck, a couple of props at the bottom and he would have a good design.

The result was *Adolescence*. Nothing he ever did pleased Grant more. He kept coming back to it for the next nine years. Originally, it was a drawing, in pencil on brown wrapping paper. He redrew it several times. Then, when he got into lithographing, he made a trial lithograph of it. Finally he did it in oil, and the painting was sold to the Abbott Laboratories at North Chicago, Illinois.

He put a limpid, innocent expression on the adolescent chicken's face, if chickens have faces, and showed it risen to its feet in the gray light of dawn. On either side of it he drew hens swollen and scowling with confusion. Perhaps a plucked chicken does not make the most appetizing picture in the world, but Grant was convinced he had made a thing of beauty of it. When the Memorial Union cafeteria at the University of Iowa wanted one of his pictures to use on the cover of a menu, he unsmilingly selected *Adolescence*. It was accepted and used.

That it was done originally on brown wrapping paper was no

indication that he considered it casual or inferior work. Out of
all the varieties and grades of paper made, he preferred exactly
what the corner grocer pulls off his roll to wrap up a package.
Grant swore there was nothing better at any price. He was likely
to develop that kind of attachment toward anything he had used
for a long time. When he was teaching later at the university, he
insisted on brown wrapping paper for his classes.

"I use nothing else," he said. "It has a fine tone and is free
from impurities. My pupils use it by the roll. It's dirt cheap. Fear
of spoiling expensive paper would cramp their style."

Later on he did *Race Horse* and *Draft Horse*, also in pencil on
brown wrapping paper, and they have been included in most
exhibits of his work. They are remarkable chiefly for line and
design, and for the overalls he put on the farmer in *Draft Horse*.
A critic once called Grant "America's greatest painter of barbed
wire." He also knew more about a pair of farmer's overalls than
any painter who ever lived.

As the fame of *Daughters of Revolution* rolled up beside that
of *American Gothic*, Grant's life began to grow complicated. In
the period before *American Gothic*, he had gone a few times to
the People's Unitarian Church (almost his only churchgoing),
and he continued to take part in the activities of a liberal group
that had formed there. He was in demand both as speaker and
dinner guest, made frequent trips, and came back with stories of
how he had been entertained in various parts of the country.

Sometimes it was suggested that he should write letters of
thanks for such entertainment, but he usually couldn't remember
his hosts' names. If someone didn't recognize *his* name, however,
he didn't like it. He once walked into the Fort Des Moines Hotel,
said he was Grant Wood and wanted a room. There was a convention of veterinarians in town and the clerk, interested in placing the delegates together, asked "Are you a veterinarian?" Grant

suffered a sudden attack of punctured ego. "I am *not* a horse doctor, and I will *go* to the Chamberlain," he said and stalked out of the hotel.

Certain of his activities increased his income, but his affairs only became more tangled. He was no businessman. It became common for artists, who seldom have a good word for a successful rival, to say that Grant Wood was no artist but a good businessman because his post-depression paintings did bring good prices,— as high as seventy-five hundred dollars—and he was paid as much as five hundred dollars a lecture on his annual tours. But in spite of this income he once borrowed money at 36 per cent interest, and he was never out of debt. It was the despair of his sponsors that when his paintings did come to be in demand, he spent his time at such things as designing a lounge chair and building a complicated exercise machine, which included a device for indoor rowing, weights to pull this way and that, and places for dumbbells and Indian clubs, all of which folded into a wall.

During the time that John Reid, who had the title of treasurer of the Stone City Art Colony, was trying to reach the seventy-five-cent settlement on approximately fifteen hundred dollars' worth of the colony's bills, Grant took the position that he was responsible in full, and paid up to whatever amount he had in his pocket.

Reid, checking here and there, never knowing whether his payment would arrive before Grant's, tried to keep track of these amounts. When he footed the thing up for the last time, it showed that Grant had spent $209.15 in out-of-pocket payments.

In Grant's final accounting to Reid, he said he was sorry to have messed up the accounts with his payments, but that owing money and being pressed to pay had made him extremely uncomfortable. He added that he could not find his receipt from the Atlantic and Pacific Tea Company of Anamosa, but was sure he had paid the bill in full, and that it was in the neighborhood of $40.00.

The Atlantic and Pacific bill to which he referred was $30.27.

More in Sorrow

THERE was no thought when the Stone City colony ended its 1933 term that the session would be its last. On the contrary, Grant and John Reid were planning to issue stock and to buy the ten acres of ground and the buildings that had been rented. The Carnegie Corporation contributed a thousand dollars to further the project.

Grant saw his colony as a permanent fixture in the midwest artistic scene as he began work on *Dinner for Threshers*, which was to have more variety of detail than anything he had done, and to be larger than his other major works.

"They put one of my pictures behind a door in Pittsburgh," he said. "They won't find a door big enough to hide this one."

It was more than six and a half feet wide (80½ inches) without its frame and eighteen and a half inches high. He made the drawing in three sections—fourteen men at a long table and two women serving in the dining room, two women over the stove in the kitchen, and a man sloshing his face with water, another combing his hair, a boy carrying water, chickens, horses, a hayrack and a barn outside. In all, the picture showed at least parts of eleven pairs of overalls.

It grew out of his recollections of the rough, heavy-eating people who came to the Wood home for threshing before his father died. One of his favorite stories was about a fine lady who sat next to him at a dinner in New York and trilled: "Oh, Mr. Wood, I do like your paintings so, especially that one *Luncheon for Threshers*."

While he was trying to complete *Dinner for Threshers,* he was made Iowa director of New Deal art projects and was appointed to lecture at the University of Iowa. Both positions took up a great deal of his time. Mrs. Wood worried about him. She was frightened, too, when some of the colony's creditors threatened to sue. She had been brought up among people who paid their bills; she treasured deeds and looked on any sort of legal trouble as a disgrace. It was she who had persuaded Grant to go—needlessly, as it turned out—to see whether he had to pay an income tax; someone had suggested possible legal difficulties. Now she thought as Vida had thought at the time when Paul was being dunned for the commercial studio rent—that Grant was getting into serious trouble.

And she thought Grant worked too hard. He had never done any physical labor for wages except in cases of severe necessity, but he would do anything at the colony—wash walls, dig trenches, repair wagons, varnish floors, cut weeds. Besides the art projects, other matters were pressing on him, and he didn't want to give up any of his interests. His speaking trips became more frequent; more people came to see him, about theatricals, about lectures, about exhibits, about contests, about newspaper and magazine articles.

The demands on his time were so numerous that Grant had to rent a studio in an old building downtown, where he could hide out now and then and get some painting done. Mrs. Wood thought the colony was too much for him. She went to Dave Turner and asked him to put a stop to this Stone City business.

Dave, too, thought that Grant ought to have more time for his painting. He wanted to oblige Mrs. Wood, who had seldom asked him to do anything. He went to Grant at 5 Turner Alley and asked him if he intended to have his colony again that year. Grant said he certainly did. They talked until both of them became short tempered. Finally Dave said: "I don't see what's the use of my furnishing you this place if you're going to throw your money away out there."

That rankled with Grant. He colored with anger and said little. Here he was, a nationally known artist, scarcely able to call his home his own—living in a hayloft, at that; and now he was being opposed in his efforts to hold a simple little summer art camp, which after all hadn't cost anybody much. Probably he didn't know until later that his mother had gone to Dave.

It was the first rift between Grant and his chief sponsor. It was a strain, not a break, in their friendship, but Dave Turner felt it deeply. He went down to his chapel and looked at Grant's paintings, mostly earlier works, which hung on the chapel walls. There was *The Cow Path*, which Grant had painted in 1922 and which hung next to the pastel-colored window he had put in the chapel. There were *The Dutchman's*, *Feeding the Chickens*, *The Horse Trader's*, *The Old Sexton's Place*, *Italian Farmyard*, or *Street in Palermo*. Dave stopped a long time in front of *Old Shoes*, which Grant had painted in 1926 and which seemed a single example of its kind. The shoes were wet, worn and lumpy; they had been set up to dry; they spoke of long hours in the open, in a drizzle of rain, on soggy ground.

Nothing could induce Turner to part with *Old Shoes*. When his children married, he let them take any painting he had except *Old Shoes* and the portrait of his father. He had forty-four Grant Wood paintings, and fourteen of Nan's, all bought when Grant needed money. It wouldn't have been possible to hold complete exhibits of Grant's work in the years that followed if Dave hadn't bought those pictures; they would have been scattered and too hard to collect.

He never let the strain in their relations stop his efforts to promote Grant Wood. He kept crating those pictures up and sending them out to exhibits; no one would go further to help out in any matter concerning Grant. Some of the exhibit catalogues looked almost as though he were the only owner of Grant Wood paintings, so often appeared the words: "Lent by David Turner, Cedar Rapids."

And he never let the strain reach a breaking point. After the rift over the Stone City colony died down, they became friendly as before. Then in 1935, when Grant ended his long stay in Turner Alley by moving from Cedar Rapids to the university seat at Iowa City, his relations with Dave again became strained. In the end, however, their friendship was re-established, as warm as ever.

Dave did write an ironic letter, when slighting remarks about him appeared in an interview attributed to Grant, but he never mailed it. For one thing, the interview referred to him as an "undertaker," and that made Dave Turner want to fight. Like other proprietors of mortuaries he wanted to be called a "funeral director"; not "undertaker," certainly, and not "mortician" either. The article stated that the Turners had bought five of Grant's pictures, to which Dave rejoined that he had forty of them, and that what was called the "intrusion of Cedar Rapids people" had been intended to help Grant when he needed help. But Dave couldn't bring himself to send the letter. What he did instead was to offer to guarantee Nan at least twenty-five dollars a month for any picture she wanted to paint for him. She replied that she didn't have enough confidence in herself to accept the regular arrangement, but that he had renewed her interest in painting and she would show him anything she did. And in 1935, when Grant was planning to move to Iowa City and was at Waubeek on the Wapsipinicon, Dave wrote to ask him to accept his apologies for any trouble he might have caused, saying they'd been friends for a long time and that he expected to hold that friendship. The letter went on to say that peace of mind is one of the greatest factors in any big success and that he didn't want to keep Grant from going to the top as soon as possible; that he realized that Grant couldn't do justice to his writing and painting with his mind on moving, buying a place and remodeling it, so to drop the whole matter.

But all that was to come later. In the spring of 1934, Grant decided he would have to give up the Stone City colony. He really was pressed for time, and money. The Carnegie Corporation was persuaded to let its thousand-dollar grant apply on old debts. John Reid handled the matter through the president of Iowa State College.

"It was the firm expectation of Mr. Wood and everyone concerned that the Stone City property would be purchased and the colony continued," the Carnegie Corporation was advised. "Since that date [July 1, 1933] several very important things have happened.

"The PWAP [Public Works of Art Project] was organized and placed under the direction of Grant Wood in Iowa. Mr. Wood has been attached to the staff of the State University of Iowa at Iowa City, and plans are under way to carry on a summer school there which will embody the best aspects of the Stone City Art Colony.

"Mr. Wood, who has been the sole sponsor of the art colony, is in debt to the amount of about $1,500 for supplies and other necessities in connection with the colony. He has been endeavoring to raise this money from several different sources and originally expected to pay it all himself.

"With increasing hard times he received no commissions and went on a very meager PWAP salary. We feel perfectly clear that the check [for a thousand dollars] should either be returned, or the expenditure of it in meeting the bills of the art colony should be authorized."

The expenditure was authorized. The statement that he "received no commissions" probably implied too much, since his paintings were always in demand after *American Gothic*, but it was true that he didn't have any money and was trying to raise it. The money didn't come in time to save the colony.

So the painted wagons were taken from Green's hill, and Green's mansion was left empty again. Paul Engle, the Iowa poet, later spent his summers there and matched his verses with the Wapsipinicon's. The wagons were close by, but they sat humbly on the ground; their wheels were gone; the last fragment of paint had weathered from them.

They were moved to an adjacent farm, operated by Frank Nissen's son, and were used as chicken houses. They were not as good for this purpose as they were for housing artists—rather low, without their wheels, and hard to get into for eggs or to clean. The chickens liked them, though, and perched on them by day besides roosting in them at night. The wagons didn't seem to mind; they were too old to look for anything better. They, and the pictures people bought, and the feeling among the farmers that maybe art wasn't a bad thing to have around, were all that remained of the Stone City colony.

With the aid of $223 contributed by John Reid, and the Carnegie money, the last of the Stone City bills were paid while Grant was finishing *Dinner for Threshers*. All were paid, that is, except three. One of these was Frank Nissen's $150 for rent. Another was a $6.08 leftover from a big lumber bill. The third was a $9.15 printing bill. There was a certain rough justice in the failure to pay that printer's bill. After all, the colony was started on a double-or-nothing arrangement with a printer; if it failed, he was not to collect.

TWENTY-FIVE

Dinner for Threshers

It is consistent with the fate of such things that *Dinner for Threshers*, born of boyhood recollections of an ordinary farm, painted in a made-over hayloft by a man who was "endeavoring to raise money," now hangs in the heart of the extensively developed Blakeford Farms, where some of the country's finest Aberdeen Angus cattle and Percheron horses are raised.

It's a two-dollar taxicab ride from the village of Queenstown, Maryland. You drive past farms on which black cows mother bulldoglike calves, and past barns with modernistic windows. The farms, covering twenty-five hundred acres, belong to George M. Moffett. There's a ten-thousand-dollar doghouse on one of these places, you are told; they raise dachshunds in it.

You turn in on a long, flat, narrow lane, lined with oak and hickory, yellow and orange and red with fall. It must be a half mile up that lane. The trees separate to show blooded horses in a field on the left and an expanse of the Chester River on the right, and at the end of the lane is the Moffetts' colonial-style house.

If gracious and charming Mrs. Moffett isn't there, Nathan, the butler, is to show you the painting. As it turns out, Mrs. Moffett is there and is awfully glad you could come. Her husband is president of a national corn products company that makes starch, syrup, Mazola and other grocery-store items.

You go into Mr. Moffett's study, to the right off the main entrance, and look around the room, leaving *Dinner for Threshers* to the last. On two walls hang Flemish portraits, two Holbeins that look like Memlings, and one van der Weyden. On the third wall is a portrait of Mrs. Moffett and on the fourth, opposite the

167

door, is *Dinner for Threshers*, in its original frame, lighted by concealed fluorescent bulbs.

You notice what doesn't always show in the prints, the year "1892" painted in large numerals on the barn-loft door. That is the year Grant used to give as the year of his birth, though he was born in 1891. Why did he pick 1892? Was it because, when he came home "a ragged failure" in 1916, he thought it would be something, at least, to be a year younger at such a low point in his life? Perhaps he changed it only because "2" is more artistic than "1." At any rate, there it is 1892, a year that meant something to him.

He did a good job with those horses in the barnyard, especially the dapple-gray reaching down for feed from a box on the ground. It's accurate, too: when the threshers come, they come with their teams and hayracks to bring the bundles of oats from the field, and with wagons to haul off the threshed grain. There's not enough room in the barns for every team, and some have to feed in the barn lot. Usually their feed would be set up on something, on a wagon or a hayrack. Grant probably wanted it on the ground so he could get more neck action in his drawing.

It was once suggested that the shadows are too directly under those chickens in the yard. They do look a little that way, but they're not. When the matter first came up, Grant got out a micrometer and produced astronomical data to prove that at noon, in his latitude, at the time of year when the threshing is done, the shadows would be exactly that much north and east of the hens. Nobody could accuse him of making a mistake concerning chickens.

The boy carrying water might be his brother Frank at the time Grant could remember him on the farm. He must be fourteen or fifteen. The face has very much the look of a Wood in youth: square, blond, a sort of peaches-and-cream innocence. The washbasin on the porch is an important item: threshers work in clouds of chaff; the stuff crawls down under your shirt and itches and mixes with sweat. When you've washed down a little below the shirt line, however, and have wet down and combed your hair, you look and feel pretty clean.

The ornamented stopper in the stovepipe hole, or flue, there in the dining room, doesn't look as though it were placed too well. The arms on those things get bent during the winter when they're lying around, not in use because the dining-room stove is up. They usually don't fit very well; Grant probably noticed this. Such small details marked his painting. You could get them in a photograph, of course, but it's different. A photograph is a photograph; a painting is part of a man's life.

The picture hanging on the wall, *Wild Horses*, or *Black and White Beauties* as Grant remembered it, that hung in almost every farmhouse he had ever been in. Then when he went to look for it, he couldn't find one. He stopped at farmhouse after farmhouse; they didn't have *Wild Horses*. They didn't have it downtown either. He was weeks getting hold of it, and nothing else would do. It was a little like not being able to find a typical farmer; one of those aggravations in the life of a painter.

Grant once said the painting included his family and his neighbors. It isn't clear who the members of his family might be. There's nobody young enough to be Jack or Nan. The woman standing behind the dining table might be his mother as he remembered her from thirty-five years before. She is more natural than the other woman; there's nothing stylized about her. None of the faces look like the daguerreotype of Maryville Wood that hangs on Frank Wood's wall. If his father is in the painting, he must be the man sitting on the piano stool, with his back turned. That would be a natural thing for the head of the house, anxious for things to go right: "Here, I'll sit on the piano stool."

Piano stool? It isn't a piano stool. It's covered with red plush and is designed for one of those old foot-powered organs. That

was what they were using for music on farms at the time Grant
was thinking of. Then came upright pianos, then talking ma-
chines, then gramophones, the victrolas, then radios. The regular dining chairs, twelve of them, are the ones his mother bought
with the money she had saved from teaching. Those are her red-
checkered tablecloths, two or three of them on such a long table.
They're using her Haviland china with the moss-rose pattern today; the ironstone dishes are on the shelves. On the floor is one
of the rag rugs Mrs. Wood kept making and giving to Grant's
friends—Dave Turner has several of them in his mortuary.

The overalls worked out well in this picture. Grant developed
his attachment to overalls long before he thought of *Dinner for
Threshers,* but things he liked had a way of fitting in when he
needed them. In this case the repetition of the X formed by over-
all straps across the farmers' backs is one of the strongest features
of the design. There are several good little portraits around the
table. The best is the man at the end, on the right. He's swallow-
ing something, holding up a cup of coffee, very busy with his eating, but he's looking up; he wants to get an eyeful of those mashed
potatoes going by. That's the way farmers eat, with an eye out
for what's coming next.

The cat there in front of the built-in kitchen cabinet—John
Reid is responsible for that cat. Reid looked at the drawing,
pointed a blunt forefinger at the space in front of the cabinet, and
said: "It needs something there." Grant put in the cat. It's a very
feline cat, puffed up about something, probably from pleasuring
the odors of the stove. When Cousin Clarabelle Weaver saw
the cat, she insisted that there ought to be a dog somewhere in the
picture, but by that time Grant was in no mood for further
changes.

And the cabinet—that's not from the farm. That's the cabinet
he built in Mrs. Wood's semibasement kitchen in Kenwood, in
the house he and Paul built, the one they moved to from the

shack. The cabinet is painted there as he built it sixteen years before, the same lines, the same knob, the same slate-bluish color. That looks like a jar of green tomato pickles on top of it, or it might be a jar of rhubarb. Grant liked rhubarb pie.

He did a lot of work on the cookstove, to get in all the twists of its ornament. Those old stoves used to be almost marks of social distinction: the woman who had the biggest cookstove with the most nickel plating had a satisfied feeling of superiority about it. Grant studied such things, even for details he couldn't use. He once sent a student out to examine a threshing machine, to see how it worked, to make sketches of its parts. The student came back with almost enough information to make a blueprint. All Grant wanted him to do was show a threshing machine in the background of a landscape.

The screen door is something you wouldn't expect to find in a Grant Wood painting. The fretwork across the corners—he always said that was senseless, a soulless travesty on all the finest principles of utility and design. But that's the kind of screen doors they had in those days. Besides, as long as you have feeling for a thing, you can paint it, whether the feeling is one of liking or of dislike.

Some people say the detail is clearer in his drawings, which have been exhibited as often as the painting. Mrs. Stanley R. Resor of New York has the complete drawing, and the two end sections that Grant redrew hang in the Whitney Museum of American Art. He got nearly two thousand dollars for the three drawings, and thirty-five hundred for the painting. He used to throw his drawings away until Miss Prescott said she would like to have them. He sent her the drawings for *Birthplace of Herbert Hoover* and *Fruits of Iowa*. Later he found the drawings could be sold, sometimes for almost as much as the paintings.

You notice that *Dinner for Threshers* is copyrighted. John Reid didn't know that. Reid had one of his lawyers look up the copyright laws and tell Grant he ought to copyright his pictures, and how to do it. Reid thought no good would ever come of it, and it didn't for several years. But when Grant came to *Dinner for Threshers* he put in his copyright mark; there is the circled *c* after "GRANT WOOD 1934." This was a "design for a mural," and he probably thought he might want to make a mural of it some day. There is no telling how long it would have taken him to paint such a mural—Leonardo worked six years on *The Last Supper*, and then didn't consider it finished. That was another day, but it would have taken Grant a lot of time. And in 1934, he didn't have much time to spare.

Professor Extraordinary

THIRTY-FOUR artists were given jobs in the studios of the PWAP at the State University of Iowa in Iowa City. Grant commuted the twenty-eight miles from Cedar Rapids to direct their work, and in this connection was engaged to give lectures three afternoons a week at the university.

Here was something to revive interest in living—the university, with its five thousand campus students in a town of seventeen thousand people, its winding walks, its solemn buildings of stone, its venerated ivy and, a half block away, a hut where you could buy very small but very good hamburger sandwiches for a nickel apiece.

At the foot of the sloping campus, on a boggy flat alongside the Iowa River, was what had been the Iowa football field, before a stadium seating fifty thousand grew in the hills on the other side of the river. On this old field Nick Kutch once outran and out-fought Red Grange, on one of Kutch's good days, and Oran Pape, an antelope while he lasted, twice snatched victory from more powerful Minnesota teams.

Beside the field was a low brick building, the old university gymnasium. Inside it, around the edges of what used to be a swimming pool, the PWAP artists worked on large designs fastened to the walls, while Grant squinted up at them and added a line here and there and consulted his original sketches.

The artists, glad to get any sort of work after the hard times of the early thirties, painted a series of mural panels for the library of Iowa State College at Ames—the agricultural school—and designed four large mural lunettes for the public library in Des

Moines. Some difficulties arose over the lunettes when a student correspondent set up a camera in the bed of the swimming pool, photographed the designs for an Iowa newspaper, and wrote an accompanying story in which he called Grant the leader of a liberal wing on the Iowa art faculty. He then listed all the members of the faculty as either liberal or conservative.

The newspaper story was intended to play up Grant as a new and progressive influence on a somewhat moss-backed faculty— as a man who would take art down off its pedestal and place it on the doorsteps of the people of the state. But the effect was to stir up wrath on the faculty and to make Grant appear to be at odds with the established authorities. And the pictures of the lunettes, showing large-armed and large-fisted men at work, brought protests from reactionaries who thought there might be something socialistic in them. The project was never carried through.

The unfavorable reaction to the lunettes was balanced by the acclaim that greeted the Ames murals. These had farming subjects, more popular in Iowa, and were based on Daniel Webster's "When tillage begins, other arts follow; the farmers therefore are the founders of human civilization."

Farming, animal husbandry, veterinary medicine, ceramics and chemistry, aeronautics and civil engineering were depicted in a progression from agriculture to the other arts. The principal scene was of a group of farmers unloading hay. The panels were exhibited as they were completed; some of them were shown at the state fair in 1934.

These murals added to Grant's already great prestige with the public, and so did several other PWAP projects—murals for University High School in Iowa City and for Harrison School in Cedar Rapids, a statue of Chief Black Hawk placed at Lake View, Iowa, eight large sculptural reliefs for the Dairy Building at Ames, and a variety of easel paintings. With John Reid on the state board of education to help matters along, Grant was made an associate professor of fine arts at the university on July 1, 1934. Before this, he had been appointed as a part-time lecturer; now he was a full member of the staff at thirty-six hundred dollars a year.

His lecture tours were also picking up at this time, and he had a good income. He bought a new car and looked prosperous. He still went without neckties in good weather, but he was carefully groomed and wore the best of ready-made clothing—usually light tweeds or rough tans, set off by two-toned shoes and a Panama or a light-felt hat. Walking about the elm-shaded campus, he made extensive plans for artistic projects to be carried out in the Grecian buildings that centered around what, before the state government was moved to Des Moines, was the Iowa Capitol Building—a masterpiece of balanced architecture.

He planned a series of frescoes for the drama department to illustrate the thirty-seven basic plots of fiction, from the struggle of man against nature and the struggle of man against man down to the eternal triangle now so well established. He thought it would take him and his students ten years to paint them. Another of his plans was for a chapel to be built on the Memorial Union grounds. He had one of his students make a model, complete with landscaping, and designed murals for it to show both the development of religious life in Iowa and the country school teaching which had been the beginning of education in the state.

He was a professor such as the university had seldom seen. One of the first things he did was to start smoking cigarettes in class. He hadn't smoked until he was nearly thirty, but by this time had become a chain smoker. He kept no record of attendance; if a student signed up for art, Grant assumed he was interested, and if the student was somewhere else during classes perhaps it was just as well.

One of his classes met in a building that had formerly been a hospital, before the state and the Rockefeller Foundation each contributed $2,250,000 to build a new medical plant. His class-

175

room had once been an operating room. One day Grant arrived late for class, wheeling an operating table in front of him. In all the new dignity of his professorship, he had thought up this way of having some fun. Paintings done by members of the class were laid flat on the operating table, and the students filed past to "operate" critically on them.

He was in Waubeek again during part of the summer of 1934, vacationing with Jay Sigmund, the poet-insurance man. Grant had smashed his new car into a milk truck and had otherwise banged it up and, shortly after leaving Grant one evening, Sigmund had an accident in which he was injured. Out of these events grew *Death on Ridge Road*, which was widely used in campaigns against highway accidents. Grant painted it first on canvas, but when it was almost completed the paint showed signs of peeling, so he redid it on panel. The painting showed a careening truck wheeling too fast around a corner, a car straddling the highway in an effort to stop, another car coming up from behind, and barbed-wire fences zigzagging into the distance on either side of the highway, which cut across barren fields—no bulbous trees. It was sold to Cole Porter, the song writer.

Dinner for Threshers was shown at the Carnegie International Exhibition at Pittsburgh in the fall of 1934 and was voted the third most popular picture in a poll taken among gallery visitors. After the exhibit, Grant went on to New York, where his fame was at its height. Christopher Morley presented him with a copy of his latest book, *Inward Ho*, inscribed it "This is for Grant Wood and so am I," and gave a dinner for him at the restaurant of the Sherlock Holmes Club. The club was a place where members wore visored caps, took their food off old-fashioned square pianos, passed into secret chambers, and worked Sherlock Holmes crossword puzzles.

Why shouldn't Iowa City have some kind of freakish club? When Grant got back to the university, he helped found the Society to Prevent Cruelty to Speakers. Clubrooms were rented for the society in a frame building over Smith's Café. It was to be a place where visiting speakers could relax, instead of attending teas and dinners. Grant undertook to decorate the clubrooms. The landlady at the place was somewhat flustered when, directing a group of men moving an old-fashioned organ into the place, she found that one of the men carrying an end of the organ was Grant Wood, the artist.

The clubrooms were done in 1890 style, with cabbage-rose wallpaper and a jig-sawed center table supporting a large plush album and a stereoscope. The furnishings included a hatrack, hair wreaths, a comb case, family group photographs, blue-plush chairs with horn arms and backs, floral pieces and a stuffed canary under bell-glass covers, and prism-heavy lamps overhead.

One of the first speakers to come to this ornate place was Thomas Benton. After duly relaxing, Benton and Grant wrote letters to Tom Yoseloff, who was president of the Times Club, the organization that had brought Benton to the campus to speak, and who was scheduled to introduce him.

Grant wrote:

"As you know I am modest to the point of being frail and therefore look to you to see that I am not embarrassed by excessive praise, no matter how true it may be. If you feel obliged to mention something about me, it might not be out of place to point out the well-known fact that American Gothic is THE outstanding American painting today.

"On second thought, perhaps that is too strong. Dinner for Threshers also is a superb painting. As for Thomas Benton's paintings, you should bring out that he has a mustache, a beautiful wife and comes from Missouri."

Benton's letter read:

"I should tip you off that America's most celebrated examples of rural painting were, by a strange coincidence, painted by me. My murals in the Whitney Museum and the Museum of Modern Art are simply staggering. My murals in the Indiana Building at the World's Fair are knockouts. This is the straight stuff.

"As for Grant Wood, I refer you to Time magazine in which I am quoted as saying: 'I know an ass and the dust of his kicking when I come across it.'"

When the speaking was over, they went back again to the Society to Prevent Cruelty to Speakers. Benton played *Frankie and Johnnie* on the harmonica, and Grant did the clog dance he had learned with Paul Hanson twenty years before. Benton later described Grant as "a middle-western painter devoid of the usual paraphernalia of sophistication."

W. C. Handy, Stephen Vincent Benét, Thomas Duncan, Sterling North, Nicholas Roosevelt, Morley, Thomas Craven and MacKinlay Kantor were among the speakers protected from cruelty in the clubrooms. Some of these, Grant met for the first time there. The society became known familiarly on the campus as the S.P.C.

TWENTY-SEVEN

The American Scene

ONE of Grant Wood's little-known achievements was to get rid of the bald spot on the back of his head. This seemingly dubious piece of information is fully verified; his barber of the time lives to vouch for it, and his later barber could tell where the spot had been.

Ward M. Coulter of Iowa City had been cutting his hair for some months when Grant asked: "Did you ever know I was bald?"

Ward hadn't noticed anything, and Grant reached up and ran a finger around the place where the vacant spot had been. Then Ward could see that, in an area bigger than a milk bottle top, the hair was of a slightly different texture.

"I had a vitamin deficiency," Grant explained. "I took pills for two years and the hair grew back."

Probably it wouldn't work for more than one man out of a thousand. But it worked for Grant, and he was a little self-satisfied about it. His hair was exceptionally fine, and his beard was light. From long habit, he shaved himself. He appeared once every two weeks, usually about 10:00 A. M., to have his hair trimmed and always gave Ward seventy-five cents for a forty-cent haircut. He liked to go without a hat, and his scalp often showed sunburn through his hair. His squint had become more pronounced, and the slight recession of his hair in front brought out his prominent forehead and high cheekbones. "Long haired" was his expression for the kind of artist he didn't like, and he was particular about how his own hair was cut. He didn't want a "Hoosier haircut," with clippers on the side; on the other hand, he wanted it trimmed up close enough so his hatband wouldn't leave a mark. After surveying himself critically in a mirror, he often asked that a little more be taken off.

He didn't talk much while his hair was being cut, but sometimes described his experiences in Paris. He never forgot those days abroad, and it was noticeable in his lectures that, while appearing on behalf of the "American Scene" movement, he spoke with feeling of his life in Paris.

A good many colleges and universities had lecture courses for which outside notables were brought in. Grant was often included on such programs, and he also gave lectures sponsored by women's clubs, art groups and various organizations. He usually was away on speaking trips during February.

His lectures always began in the same way. He spoke of how he liked to draw as a child, and how he continued to draw and paint while he was growing up.

"When I was a youngster a person had no chance as a painter in this country unless he had European training," he would say. "The romantic French and Italian styles were the most popular. Painting in those days was separated entirely from life. Painters were considered so different from other men that they were pretty generally thought to be sissies.

"In consequence of this American attitude, I went to France to study and did a thorough job of becoming French. Due to my cultivation of Gallic tastes I was very much at outs with the midwest when I returned to the United States."

His most quoted remark was: "I suddenly realized that all the good ideas I ever had came to me while I was milking a cow." It is a symbolic statement: he didn't spend much time milking cows. But it was the point he always worked up to in his lectures—the change that began to evolve in his work after his return from Paris in 1926.

He didn't claim to have started any movement. "American

painting was undergoing significant changes, and I started to change also," he said, and in answer to some of the more extravagant claims for him added: "I didn't really discover America. That's too broad a proposition for a fellow like me. But I did return from my third trip to France to see, like a revelation, my neighbors in Cedar Rapids, their clothes, their homes, their tablecloths and curtains, the tools that they used. I suddenly saw all this commonplace stuff as material for art—wonderful material."

Neither American subjects nor narrative painting were really new to him at that time. Although he had produced many French and Italian scenes in the middle twenties, *Looking for Wigglers, The Horse Trader's,* and *Grandma's Place,* all earlier paintings, were narrative and as American as they could be. The earlier paintings, however, were done in a generally accepted style. There was more conviction behind his work after 1926. He was older; apprehensive ambition with its desire to conform didn't rise up to choke his self-confidence and originality; he had the patience to build large by piling up small detail, and the courage to use hard lines and what he called "decorative" effects—some of which he got from Dave Turner's collection of Currier & Ives.

"Interpreting the commonplace" was the best expression for what Grant started to do, but even that was too scholarly to indicate what really happened. When Grant was trying to recall exactly how it was that he changed, he told of returning from Paris, fed up with all the fine talk and useless gesturing connected with his one-man show, and of seeing his mother in the doorway. And the thought that then crossed his mind was: "This is the thing."

It was as simple as that. All the elaborate talk about his return to the soil, his discovery of the American scene, his throwing off European ventriloquism and building a native art came along years later. The real story was that a man went out to paint the world and came back home and found that the life and living he had left were not much different from what they were elsewhere, that they were better known and understood by him, and equally worth painting.

Grant himself, in his lectures, carried the story much further, developing the idea of regionalism. His basic theme was that a man should paint the thing he knew best. Reasoning from that point, he said that a man's experience ordinarily would be rooted in a particular area, which meant that he would do his painting close to home. This, in turn, meant that regional art centers would spring up, and they would naturally compete with each other.

No regions were ever defined, and no regional centers were ever designated. If anybody wanted to know what regionalism was, it was simply this: it would be a good idea if artists painted close to home and if there were regional centers where they could show their work.

"The hope of building a native American art," Grant said, "lies in the development of regional art centers and competition among them."

He was called a regional artist until he almost regretted having mentioned the subject. As early as 1934, he was beginning to be annoyed by the effects of this movement and the interpretations put on it.

"Too many people, young fellows all over the country, are trying to climb on this bandwagon of what they call regionalism," he said. "They're mistaking the superficial mannerisms of John Curry or of Tom Benton or of myself for the real thing. As a matter of fact, I'm trying mighty hard to get rid of those early mannerisms. I'm doing everything I can to forget them."

He was objecting to the fact that young artists seemed to think regionalism consisted of painting bulbous trees and fat hills. Such things usually did not survive the transfer from one artist to another—the feeling in them was lost along the way. Besides, the chief purpose of the movement was to encourage the individual artist to paint what he himself knew best, not what he borrowed from someone else.

Some pretty terrible paintings were being turned out. "The critics of regional art," Grant said, "will look at these pictures and come to us and say 'See what you are doing. This is all your fault.' The same artists who did fake impressionist pictures in Paris a few years ago are now busy on the American scene. God save it from them."

When the formal part of his lectures was over, Grant brought out colored slides of his own paintings and threw them on a screen. Members of the audience were permitted to ask questions. About *Birthplace of Herbert Hoover,* for instance, someone would ask why his picture didn't look like the birthplace itself. Grant would explain that if you wanted to duplicate a thing, you took a camera; that his object was to create a design, to heighten effects, to present an idealized version.

On the other side of this question, someone would ask what was the difference between his art and abstractionism. Grant's reply was that with all their departures his pictures still had their roots in reality, and that he didn't believe art could otherwise be made understandable to a large public.

"Art can be a significant form of expression, understandable to virtually everyone, and still not violate basic esthetic principles," he said. "Art need not be the exclusive property of the intelligentsia, as so many of the surrealists and post-impressionists seem to think. They are very bitter about our work."

Grant's position was subject to attack at times. His attempts to persuade artists to throw off European influences ran up against the fact that European influences were apparent in all his own work. And although it was a natural conclusion from his argument that time spent away from home was more or less wasted, he himself undoubtedly saw Cedar Rapids more clearly because he had been away from it a good deal.

"Interpreting the commonplace" didn't sound like a nationalistic idea, but it naturally involved recognizably American settings and Grant's following came to include people who were not so much attracted by his work as they were by the thought of creating a purely American art. There were among them some who had no liking for the common people he painted, or the people he painted for. Grant fell in, to some extent, with the nationalistic trend.

"America has at last found a type of painting all its own," he declared. "It has finally broken away from Europe and discovered its own way of expression."

But he was sometimes a little dazed and skeptical about it all.

"They are trying to make me a glamour boy of American art," he said. "Actually I'm the plainest kind of fellow you can find. There isn't a single thing I've done, or experienced, that's ever been the least bit exciting."

Fame and Red Flannels

TEACHING at the university didn't require much of Grant's time. He never had the title of resident artist, but was given a light schedule—he was in his classroom nine hours a week—and this was not to interfere with his painting. In the winter of 1934–35 he was planning another picture: "The Bath, 1880."

In the center of the picture was to be a round wooden tub, the kind he had used in his silversmith days at the Wolund Shop. In the background would hang vivid, blue-checked aprons. And beside the tub was to stand a man clad in red-flannel underwear, with a grim look of distaste on his face. People considered in 1880 that you took a bath at considerable risk, that it was a sort of short cut to pneumonia. It was customary afterward to rub the chest vigorously with a corncob, to ward off disease.

Only one thing was holding up the painting: Grant couldn't find a satisfactory suit of red-flannel underwear. He needed one that was showing its age, baggy at the knees and elbows and faded out a little here and there. So on January 6, 1935, he advertised in newspapers in Iowa, Illinois and Minnesota for a suit of red-flannel underwear, vintage 1880, must be well worn and authentic.

Replies came in from persons anxious to be helpful. At first they weren't encouraging. One woman wrote that she couldn't find the bottoms, but she had two red-flannel tops; would those do? Another said she had a red-flannel petticoat and could make it over for him if that would be all right. Grant continued to insist on the genuine article.

"You have no idea how near being a museum piece this type

of undergarment has become," he said. "The disappearing buffalo has nothing on red flannels."

He was in a good humor. His fame had risen steadily, his professorship had added cultural status, his income, by comparison
with the past, was large; he was still living at 5 Turner Alley and
seeing paintings ahead. Besides "The Bath, 1880," he was thinking of a "Balloon Ascension" at a county fair, with all the gaping
and neck craning that would involve, and of doing something with
an old fiddlers' contest.

An authentic suit of worn red flannels was finally found. At the
same time, an ominous note began to appear in the criticism of
Grant's work. Critics had called him an Iowa Moses; now they
found him a man of minor talent, an inhibited craftsman. Docu-
mentary, tiresome, jejune, irritating, puerile, photographic and
mediocre were some of the adjectives applied to his painting. His
emphasis on subject matter was heavily scored.

He was called a meteor that had flashed big in the sky and then
sputtered down dismally. "Grant Wood has become a popular,
almost mythical figure," wrote one critic. "His success has been
too sudden, too hot-house to be robust." "This artist's social comments," said another, "are expressed through portraits of Revolutionary Daughters and Victorian Survivals. They belong to a
school of caricature which is extremely obvious."

Grant's place at the university was not too secure. While he
had good friends, there were those who disagreed seriously with
him on art and on teaching methods, those who were sophisticated and didn't like his simplicity, and those who were dignified
and didn't like his antics. The fact that he was a recognized and
accepted artist was what got him on and kept him on the staff—
something he never forgot. If he were to fall from grace in the
world of art, there would be fellow faculty members to help pull
him down.

What set off his detractors more than anything else was his

advertising for those red flannels. Undoubtedly Grant was aware of the publicity value of this move. "The Bath, 1880" was to be for people who would see human and humorous angles in such a painting, and advertising was a good way of letting them know it was coming. Reporters wrote feature stories, "Painter Looking for Underwear," and the stage was properly set.

But in every artistic circle there are people who pronounce "publicity seeker" with venom, even though the publicity sought is for the purpose of arousing wider interest in works of art. They called Grant a publicity seeker in the kind of sentences that bend in the middle and slap you in the face with both ends.

Grant let it get under his skin. It was all very well to be popular with the public, but an artist must belong to his profession, to his clan. What was the use of being on the cover of *Liberty* magazine if the art magazines, the magazines he read, treated him with but thinly veiled disdain?

He abandoned "The Bath, 1880," and everything connected with it. He issued a statement that he was deeply worried, that he wasn't seeking and didn't need publicity, and that he was more interested in teaching than he was in painting. He signed a contract to write a book on American art. He stopped painting altogether for more than a year, and didn't get back to steady painting for more than four years.

And he got married. Soon after his appointment to the university, he began to show an interest in marriage. When he returned from his trip to New York in the fall of 1934 he told John Reid:

"John, I've met someone who I think is the person."

"Is it mutual?"

"Yes."

"Are you sure?"

"Yes, I'm sure. As soon as it can be worked out, I think something will come of it."

Reid didn't know to whom he was referring, but later Grant's evenings began to be taken up. Reid would call up suggesting a movie, and Grant, bland as always, anxious to please everybody, would say: "I can go, John, if you'll go to the first show, but I've got an engagement at 9:15."

His engagements were with Sara Sherman Maxon, a striking, handsome woman with white hair and erect carriage. Like Grant, she had been born in Jones County, adjacent to Linn, the county that includes Cedar Rapids, and like him she had artistic interests.

She had studied voice in Chicago, had sung as a leading contralto in Reginald De Koven's light-opera company in New York, and had toured the east as a lieder singer. At the time, she was directing the Women's Club Chorus in Cedar Rapids and the Jones County Farm Bureau Chorus, and was giving voice lessons.

Mrs. Wood was ill that winter, and Sara often came to 5 Turner Alley to look after her. Since Grant had to be away a good deal, this attention was greatly appreciated. He and Sara were seen together often, and there began to be rumors of a marriage. Grant made no denials, and the news got into the Gazette.

It was the subject of considerable talk in Cedar Rapids. Grant was regarded almost as a piece of municipal property, like a monument in the park, and the impression was general that he wouldn't look out for his own interests. After David Turner began getting people to buy his paintings, Grant used to protest that they weren't worth what was being paid for them—Dave had set prices on more of the pictures than Grant had. There were always people looking after his affairs for him.

So when it became known that he was planning to marry, it was looked upon as a matter of general concern, and some of his friends and sponsors opposed it. They wanted him to marry someone younger, someone considerably younger than himself, and perhaps yet have a family. Grant was forty-four; Sara was forty-nine.

Turner said what he could against the marriage. John Reid gave a dinner to which he invited Grant and some of his friends, the purpose being a joint effort to dissuade him from his intentions. Grant forestalled it all by announcing his engagement before the dinner was well started. He told those who approached him privately on the subject that he had been thinking the matter over for months, and had made up his mind. Artists were funny people, he admitted, but since he and Sara were both artistic he was sure they would understand each other and get along well.

Grant bought Sara's ring at the Kalo Shop in Chicago. Twenty years after he had worked there for sixteen dollars a week, he went back as a painter and professor and gave detailed instructions as to what he wanted made: a diamond between two oblong amethysts.

By walking a block to the Kalo workshop, he could have seen Daniel Pedersen, who had lived with him in the farmhouse out in Park Ridge, and other craftsmen he had worked with. He didn't do it. He only went to the showrooms on Michigan Avenue, just south of the Art Institute.

He was planning to marry, and didn't have much time, and didn't know who was still working at Kalo's—there were plenty of reasons for not visiting the workshop. In any case, it wouldn't have been like him to look up people he hadn't seen for nineteen or twenty years. He was the kind of person to whom things happened, without his going out of his way, and his attachments were to whatever chance placed close at hand.

Except for his family and a few with whom he was in close contact, his deepest feelings didn't attach themselves to human beings. They lingered a long time over corn shocks and plowed furrows and the roll of the ground, and their last refuge was in design.

"I think he was a little conceited," said one of the Kalo designers. "He never had anything to do with the rest of us. He was always by himself."

The wedding plans were kept secret. Grant told a few friends when it would be and wrote letters to others, but there was no announcement. He and Sara were married on March 2, 1935, in Minneapolis, at the home of Dr. Sherman Maxon, a dentist, Sara's son by a previous marriage. They would be at home in Cedar Rapids after May 1.

Not Single Spies

To GET some time for the book he was to write on American art, Grant established himself in a farmhouse at Waubeek—a small cluster of houses on the Wapsipinicon. With him were Sara, his mother, and Park Rinard, a young University of Iowa graduate whom he engaged as a secretary and who was to be coauthor of the book.

No. 5 Turner Alley had but a single entrance, and Grant said he wanted a place with a back door he could get out of, "so the family can truthfully report me missing." In his youth he had put writing on a level with painting among his ambitions, and he was anxious to do a good job with the book.

It was sometimes called his autobiography and sometimes a cowritten biography, although from the first he planned to bring in Benton, Curry and the whole American Scene movement. Like his lectures, it was to be built around his own life, and to stress the use of home subjects in painting.

"All I shall contend for," he said, "is the sincere use of native materials by the artist who is in command of them."

In February, 1935, he had had an exhibition of his paintings at the Lakeside Press Galleries in Chicago, and in April he had a one-man show in New York, at the Ferargil Galleries. It was the first time his work had been exhibited in New York, and the critics and special writers expressed amazement that he had reached fame without passing through the New York turnstiles. Grant arrived two weeks late for his New York exhibit—one way of showing that he didn't consider it important.

There were sixty-seven paintings in the exhibition, a great number of them lent by David Turner. Of all the paintings he had done, Grant at this time owned only five, including the little water color *Currants*. At the exhibit, only two early works were for sale—it was commonly said there was nothing for sale. Grant had only prestige to gain.

His scale of living now was far different from what it had been during those concentrated years in the alley when he was painting steadily. It had been a long time since he had done any interior decorating. Soon after his marriage, he was elected to the National Academy of Design, and later to the National Society of Mural Painters.

For a time it looked as though he might emerge as a radio figure. Letters were exchanged on the subject of getting him a national radio program, but nothing ever came of the project. His sponsors opposed it on the usual grounds: he ought to be painting.

His letters to critics had formerly been almost timid; he mildly took them to task and asked "Would you please explain? It isn't clear," and this timidity had been characteristic of his manner of speaking as well. Now with a secretary at his side, he wrote in a stronger style. *Time* magazine had reproduced *Dinner for Threshers* and readers had written in to criticize various details. In August, 1935, Grant replied:

"*Dinner for Threshers* is from my own life. It includes my family and our neighbors, our tablecloths, our chairs, and our hens. It was painted with my paint and my brushes on my own time. It is of and by me, and readers have no right to try to force upon me their families and their farms."

Most of the objections were that things on the farm weren't exactly as he had pictured them. One woman pointed out that there was no screen on the "back" door, and that the place should be full of flies. To this Grant replied:

Courtesy of Jo Hennessey

SPRING TURNING

ADOLESCENCE

"Why allow me, without comment, to bisect an entire house and then quibble about a screen door? Especially when the presence of the screen door would ruin my composition. If the lady from North Dakota is so mentally hide-bound that she cannot make allowance for this, let her imagine the screen door open at a 45 degree angle—for a momentary and flyless space of time."

He was planning to move to Iowa City, and was attracted by an old brick house at 1142 East Court Street, in a neighborhood peopled chiefly by retired farmers and businessmen. It had been built in 1858 by Nicholas Oakes, who, hard-bitten and bearded, walked the sixty-five miles from Davenport to establish Iowa City's first brickyard. The house had eleven rooms and brick walls twenty-six inches thick, but had been long vacant and was in melancholy condition. The more Grant saw what was wrong with the house, the better he liked it—he was attracted by the possibilities for improvement. He began to think seriously of buying the property.

It was at this time that Dave Turner wrote him at Waubeek that "peace of mind is one of the greatest factors in any big success" and "you can't do justice to your writing and painting with your mind thinking about moving." "Cedar Rapids *is* a darned good town and people here *do* appreciate you and do want you to succeed," Dave wrote.

If Grant decided to move to Iowa City, Turner's daughter and her husband planned to move into 5 Turner Alley. Dave wrote Grant that he had talked to them, that they were ready to make other arrangements, and "you are most welcome to 5 Turner Alley until July 1, 1936."

Grant sat down and tried to write Dave a friendly letter. He said he realized that the offer was meant with all the kindness in the world, but he did not wish or intend to remain in Turner Alley for another year, but only to be allowed to use the studio until September 15, as at first agreed.

And he was still thinking of their rift over the Stone City colony. He cast up the balance between him and Dave and called attention to the fact that what had been only storage space had become a rentable property, made by his own efforts from a hayloft. He said it had cost him four thousand dollars, not counting his labor, and that from the last thousand dollars, for remodeling the storeroom into a shop, he had had almost no benefit, so recent had been the improvement. As for rental, he thought that had been fairly well taken care of by his doing odd jobs for the Turner firm and family. He even thought the balance was such that Dave should pay two leftover bills, one for plumbing and another for picture framing.

He tried to close in a friendly way by saying that he had valued Dave's friendship over the years, but then he added what seemed scarcely the note to strike regarding an arrangement that had been based on personal liking and a desire to help an artist—that he was trying to show his appreciation in a practical way.

Relations between Grant and Dave Turner thus remained formally correct, and yet strained. Grant's feelings on the subject seemed to go up and down. On the day of his marriage, after a talk with Miss Prescott in which she reminded him how Dave Turner had helped him and rallied support for him through lean years, he wrote Dave a letter warmly expressing his appreciation. At other times, Grant remembered their differences, and the thoughts rankled. On one occasion he said: "Dave Turner bought my pictures because he knew they'd be worth a lot of money some day."

Grant bought the Iowa City house for thirty-five hundred dollars on a mortgage. Cedar Rapids people were sorry to lose him. They thought things wouldn't be the same without him there in the alley, and some of his friendships were broken, or strained, or simply dropped. It was a strange thing for a man to be taking leave of an entire population, but in a place like Cedar Rapids, you really can almost belong to the town.

While the move was in progress, Mrs. Wood stayed on at Waubeek. She sat on the porch of the farmhouse and looked at the Wapsipinicon. She was getting very old; this was to be her last summer. To her, Grant was hardly yet a man. Sometimes when visitors were gathered around him, she would be seen sitting off at the side. One of the visitors, going over to engage her in conversation, would praise the draftsmanship and tonal harmony of one of Grant's paintings. Mrs. Wood would respond by looking in Grant's direction and saying: "Yes, Grant is a fine boy." She became very ill in the late summer, and was taken to Iowa City, where she lived on into October.

On October 9, 1935, it was announced from Washington that a commission to paint some murals in the courthouse at Cedar Rapids had been awarded to Francis Robert White, a twenty-eight-year-old graduate of the Pennsylvania Academy of Fine Arts. That any public murals should be painted in Cedar Rapids without Grant Wood being mentioned in connection with them was so startling that reporters called him up from all over the state to ask what was the matter. Grant told them, "It's the first time I've heard of the courthouse murals."

In a rash of announcements, he added that he was turning down an appointment as regional director for federal relief of artists in five states, and was rejecting a commission granted him to paint a mural in the post office at Washington. He had already taken samples of the marble for the Washington mural, which was to have been for the west end of the Benjamin Franklin Postal Station; now he said he was too busy to carry it through.

Two days later, on October 11, Grant called the Frank Woods in Waterloo to say that Mrs. Wood was sinking: she might last only a few hours, or it might be two weeks. He had to call back the same day, while they were getting ready to come, to say that she was gone. Nan was in Texas and couldn't get there. Jack was ill. Only Grant was at her side.

When Mrs. Wood was in the last stages of her illness, she asked to see Vida Hanson. Perhaps, after all, the days she remembered best were those spent in the shack, and in hunting with Vida through the hazel brush for elderberries. Grant sent word to Vida, who drove to Iowa City and with some difficulty found the Grant Wood residence. She was told at the door that Mrs. Wood was too ill to receive a visitor; her trip had been for nothing.

Vida felt badly about that. She wanted to see "Woody" again before she died. She wanted to see Grant, too; she had something to tell him. When Vida's son Bob was a baby, she had heard that if you drew your fingers across the top of a baby's head from front to back, its hair would come out curly. Without believing it too much, she kept doing it, absent-mindedly, while Bob was sitting on her lap. Grant kidded her about it, especially after Bob's hair came out straight as a string. He had made the Hansons a bookplate, "Paul & Vida . . . Their Book," on which he pictured a fat baby with an even procession of curls across the top of its head —only on top of its head, no curls anywhere else. The bookplate kept reminding them of it, and it lived as a joke between them for years. Grant would open a book, and glance at Bob's straight hair, and grin at Vida. Vida would smile, remembering the days when Bob was an infant and Grant had made the mother-and-child.

Then when Grant was moving in other spheres and Bob reached the age of seventeen and began to use oil preparations on his hair, it suddenly became curly. He developed a regular marcel wave.

Vida thought Grant would have been interested in that. She never did get a chance to tell him.

THIRTY

A Little Earth

CLARENCE WOOD, Maryville's bachelor brother, took over the old family place. He farmed the black soil for which Joseph Wood paid three dollars an acre, and during the first World War sold hogs for a thousand dollars a carload. Then he sold the farm for three hundred dollars an acre, and retired. As age advanced upon him, he wanted to do something to set off the Wood family cemetery lot in Anamosa. He installed a huge monument, topped by a lion.

That lion was the bane of Grant's existence. He liked the kind of lions that roll over and purr in Shavian plays, but this monstrous beast of stone grated on every artistic nerve in his being.

Uncle Clarence didn't spare·expense; there must be ten tons of that monument. The lion is fully eight feet long. Its great mane stands up in frozen curlicues, and it has a long, smug nose resting on its forepaws. It is supposed to be asleep, but it looks more as though it were playing possum, and perhaps eyeing the graves through half-closed lids. Grant used to stand grimly before it, his arms folded, his jaw set, and then utter one soul-stirring word: "Horrors."

To make matters worse, Uncle Clarence told everybody that Grant had designed the monument. Uncle Clarence meant this merely as an extra homey touch, with no damage intended to the truth; it sounded better than saying he had hired a commercial tombstone designer. But Grant ground his teeth every time the story came back to him. In exasperation, he would say: "There has never been a lion in the Wood family." Or rather, as he would drag out and emphasize it:

"There has—*never*—been—a—*lion*—in the Wood—family."

197

Grant's hatred of the lion was a family joke, and even he smiled wryly about it. But as an artistic matter, it was also serious with him. When Mrs. Wood died, he showed how serious it was. In his grief over her loss it became fixed in his mind that there was still one thing he could do: he wouldn't let his mother be buried in the Wood family cemetery lot, not while that lion was there.

Others in the family wanted to bury her next to Maryville. It seemed to them both customary and right. Grant wouldn't have it, and since no one else's feelings on the subject were as strong as his, he had his way. Mrs. Wood, into whose face millions have looked and will look—though she never wanted any such distinction—was buried instead in the Weaver family lot, on the edge of a roadway that skirts the Wapsipinicon.

She never meant to stir up that ache you feel for the passing years when you look at her portrait. No woman could have been more willing to remain obscure, and it was only chance that she reminded so many of aging mothers at home. She wanted only to live and to hold her head up, to make rag rugs and to see her children well and established—and to see Grant have what he wanted, an artist's career.

Probably her life was no harder than most. Like everyone else, she hated to see the years carry off things she had held to; then something would happen to raise her spirits, and this was too bad, and that was fine. Things did pile up on her toward the last, though. She was ill a good deal, and a sort of artistic whirlpool formed with Grant at its center. She was too old to adjust herself or to find a clear way for him in all that was happening.

It wasn't her life that was being lived during those eleven years at 5 Turner Alley. Even people who visited in the alley for years didn't know what kind of person she was, except that she was plain and quiet and quaint and seldom went anywhere. It was out on Northeast Fourteenth Street and in Kenwood, when her children were still growing up and relying on her, and back in Anamosa, where she was taken to be buried, that she was really a part of what was going on—riding to town with her father, on a board stretched across a wagon box; attending box socials, teaching, and going with Maryville Wood, who was thirty years old, and had a farm, and had been living out there too long alone.

She was seventy-seven years old when she died. The body was sent to the Turner mortuary. Funeral services were simple and brief. She was buried not far from her husband—because Joseph Wood and DeVolson Weaver had bought adjacent cemetery lots, back when Anamosa was little more than a trading post. Grant's relatives on both sides of the house were buried within a few feet of each other. That was one of the many things he didn't like about Clarence's big monument: it was too close to the Weaver stone, which is modest and plain.

Mrs. Wood was placed farthest from the monuments, which are up from the road, at the back of lots that are nine graves deep. A small evergreen tree, tougher than it looks, grows out of the roadbank. It has knotted its muscles against the winds that sweep down the valley, and stretches thin, crooked branches over the spot where lies this woman who had a son who absorbed more than most from what was around him, a son who saw where others only looked, and who told what he saw in pictures.

Grant wasn't painting in the months that followed Mrs. Wood's death. He was teaching, lecturing and working on the book. A second death in the family followed two months later when his brother Jack died at the age of forty-two. Grant's break with Cedar Rapids had just fully materialized: like almost everything else in his life, it came about gradually. His chief interest was the old house in Iowa City.

There was something about the past that attracted him; a good part of his life was spent in recalling, preserving and restoring. He liked this old brick house, as plain and straight-up-and-down as a small boy's drawing, because it was the kind of thing people were building seventy-five or a hundred years before. Some occupant, after Nicholas Oakes, had built a full-length porch across the front in an effort to relieve its severity. That wasn't what Grant wanted. He tore off the porch and set out to make the place more true to its day.

He studied old photographs and found that someone had removed the original dentil work from under the eaves. He had that put back. He refurbished some old iron stars that had been covered by the porch. He did research to find how numerals were usually formed in 1850, and painted the address in that style on a stone in the yard. He discarded the pump and restored a bucket lift in the cistern next to the back door.

Modern improvements went in at the same time. He had a concrete-reinforced retaining wall built against his nearest neighbor's lot, which was on a somewhat higher level. He installed an expensive oil burner. After all these years he wasn't going to suffer from the cold again, as he had in his youth.

When he first moved to the house, he had pulled up all the red and pink hollyhocks that grew around it. People should know that such things clashed with the brick. He set out bleeding hearts, delphiniums, peonies, roses and lilacs, and a row of coral bells the full 102-foot length of the yard. He landscaped with evergreen trees, but kept a moping, flat-headed willow that drooped over the front lawn. He had the driveway put into sod: he didn't want cars standing in a driveway to clutter the view.

Sara had a girl to do the kitchen work, and Park Rinard moved to the house after Mrs. Wood's death. Entertaining at the Grant Wood residence was sometimes lavish. On one occasion, the day of a home-coming football game at the university, two turkeys were on the table, and the guests came out in a chartered bus. Nine of them stayed overnight. Noted people, like Carl Sandburg and

Lawrence Tibbett, as well as painters, stopped to share in the hospitality.

Visitors from Cedar Rapids weren't always welcome. There were exceptions, but a number who knocked at his door were told that Grant was too busy to see them. Cedar Rapids people thought that marriage, the university, the cultured society and the important people with whom he was mingling must have made a difference in Grant. They spoke of him during this period as "Grant under the Influence." The explanation given was that "the artist must have time to work." That was one reason for leaving Cedar Rapids; too many people came to see him. Actually, he now had more guests than ever before.

He may have felt out of place at some of his large entertainments. He was used to a studio with low sloping roofs and dormer windows, and to his mother, who didn't move around much. Sometimes when his house was full of guests, passers-by would see him standing behind a corner of the house, hatless, his suit coat collar turned up if the night was cold, having a cigarette or a highball by himself.

There on the other side of that flat-headed willow stood a man who had arrived, an artist, a professor, a man often sought out for the loan of his name. It had seemed to him in Cedar Rapids that he wasn't fully appreciated, that success wasn't paying out the dividends he had imagined it would. So he had left Cedar Rapids, fixed up a house, had guests and tried to fit into a new cultural pattern. Now what he wanted was a small piece of solitude, even if it had to be in the cold.

Main Street

HAVING an artist at 1142 East Court Street livened the conversation considerably in that vicinity. Grant had chosen to settle in a section where there were few university people. At first it was thought that high living was in progress in the old Oakes place, since its lights burned long after others went out. Then it was learned that a strange, mild and somehow defenseless man was living there—a man who sometimes appeared on doorsteps asking people to pose, or to dig into their grandmother's trunk for curtains, gowns, veils or hoods he could use in his drawings. He made polite remarks about the weather, and explained that the drawings were for book illustrations.

Grant emerged as an illustrator in the spring of 1936. His detractors said he was now "in the frank role of illustrator," implying that it wasn't much change from what he had been doing. To others, it seemed a minor role for a painter of lasting works in oil, though plenty of artists have followed the same route. He had become discouraged with painting, and illustrating was a good way to make money, which, as the owner of a big house, he needed now. Instead of spending months and years producing a painting, he now spent a mere matter of days and weeks over a drawing.

His chief projects were two series of drawings, one for *Farm on the Hill*, a child's book by Madeline Darrough Horn, wife of a university professor, and the other for a special, limited edition of Sinclair Lewis' *Main Street*. The farm drawings were suited to a story of a city boy's experiences on a farm. There were eight large decorative drawings in colored pencil, under such titles as *Boy Milking Cow*, *Grandma Mending*, *Grandpa with Popcorn*,

and *Boy Taking Bath,* along with twelve small humorous drawings of farm animals. All the drawings were in the style of *Fruits
of Iowa,* artistic and humorous but without showing much individuality or character in the subjects. When they were exhibited
at the Walker Galleries in New York during May of 1936, one
of the critics called them "simple, wooden figures, most excel-
lently drawn with innumerable and almost invisible little pencil
strokes, and almost completely devoid of emotional force and
vitality."

The *Main Street* illustrations interested him more. He had been
an admirer of the book. "It is a fact," he said, "that an upsurge of
painting follows an upsurge of writing. Sinclair Lewis' *Main Street*
and *Babbitt* opened the middlewest for the painter." And he used
actual models, easily recognizable, to represent types in the book
—*The Perfectionist, Sentimental Yearner, The Radical, The
Good Influence, Practical Idealist* and *Booster.*

If you knew the people who posed for him, it was sometimes
difficult to see in them the types they were considered to represent. *The Booster,* for instance, didn't look like a booster; it looked
like Professor Frank Luther Mott, posing as a booster, and a little
amused by the procedure. For *The Radical* Grant used Sara's son,
Dr. Sherman Maxon, who became a member of the university
staff and was living with his wife and child at Grant's place. To
Sherman's face he added a waxed and carefully twisted mustache
which it is hard to imagine as having anything to do with radicals,
but the individuality of the subject made it an interesting picture.
The drawing that attracted the most attention was *The Good
Influence,* the model for which was Mrs. Mollie Green, hostess
at Iowa City's leading hotel. Grant drew her once with a solemn,
brooding expression, and once with a benevolent smile. Then he
put them together, using the eyes of the first drawing with the
smile of the second—a device that Leonardo is supposed to have
found useful. The result was a benevolent expression, but with a

startling quality, too—a suggestion of suffering behind the serene exterior.

Fifteen hundred copies of the special edition of *Main Street* were printed at the Lakeside Press in Chicago by the Limited Editions Club. Besides the portraits, the book contained three other drawings—*General Practitioner*, a study of a doctor's hands, *Main Street Mansion*, a big-porched old house, and *Village Slums*, a well and a pump surrounded by outhouses, with paths through the snow leading from houses jammed together. Pages were sent to Grant from Chicago and, with an old-fashioned pen, he signed each copy of the book.

Some of his time in 1936 went to designing book jackets. Back in 1933 and 1934, he had designed covers for two of Vardis Fisher's novels, *Passion Spins the Plot* and *In Tragic Life*. Now he made jackets for *Plowing on Sunday* by Sterling North and *O, Chautauqua* by Thomas Duncan. The Chautauqua book gave him a chance to create an effective design, taking an aerial view of a Chautauqua tent, and some liberties with the tent ropes.

He became coauthor with Jewell Bothwell Tull of the one-act play *They That Mourn*. Grant's principal contributions were his name and the leading character—a man who liked to fool with mechanics and to fish, but whose wife was a prim churchgoer who badgered him into proper pursuits, so that when she died his principal thought was that now for the first time in his life he could buy himself a bicycle.

Grant's painting seemed far away while all this was going on. But he had a painting in progress. He set out with more than his usual care to create a landscape. In the past he had often made clay models of plowed furrows, to study the shadows from different angles. This time he made a complete model in clay of his landscape, to get depth and scale. He dotted the model with inch-high milkweeds and two-inch fence posts.

Like a man with a hobby that he pursues for relaxation, he worked over this model until the scene was as complete as any that could be seen from a hilltop. Those in Paris who had laughed at him for planning his pictures so carefully in advance should have seen this meticulous procedure. When the model was done he painted *Spring Turning,* his first painting in nearly eighteen months.

The people who had stared out from his paintings were long since gone. So were the fat trees. Even the roll of the ground was not important in this painting. The hand plows and figures walking behind them were too small to carry much of the picture; the tool shed and windmill were obscure at the left. His feeling was for the design, for the arrangement of squares made possible by partly plowed fields with heavy black edges. It was designed so powerfully that the fields seemed to move up and down to get into balance from whatever angle you looked at the painting. It was hung in the Walker Galleries in September, 1936, and was bought by the late Alexander Woollcott.

In June, 1936, Grant received his first honorary degree. Similar degrees were to follow in later years. So it happened that a man who in 1912 couldn't pass the Iowa teachers' examination became a Doctor of Letters, University of Wisconsin; a Master of Arts, Wesleyan University; a Doctor of Fine Arts, Lawrence College; and a Doctor of Fine Arts, Northwestern University. Grant made a drawing in which he pictured himself receiving such a degree. He appeared to be about a foot and a half shorter than the solemn, robed figures on either side of him, and seemed in a bemused way to be wishing there were some means of escape. He later used the drawing for a lithograph—he began lithographing in 1937—and titled it *Honorary Degree.*

The book on which he and Park Rinard were working was reported to be getting at least into rough shape, after two false starts.

Then Thomas Benton gave up teaching in the east and went back to Missouri with the explanation that he had been "talking too much." Grant admitted that American Scene regionalism "has reached the point where it needs nothing so much as four-wheel brakes." It was no time to bring out a book on the subject.

He and Rinard kept working on the book from time to time. Strangely enough, even recounting the details of Grant's own life involved difficulties. There was a dramatized version of his life that had been printed over and over. It went something like this: He was the son of a Quaker farmer and was born in strict Victorian surroundings; as a boy, he had to hide under the table to draw; when he was ten years old, his father died and from then on he worked like a nailer to support the family; despite this, he studied art at night and broke with his Victorian background; when the family was completely impoverished, he bought a lot for a dollar down and built a ten-by-sixteen-foot shack in which he and his mother lived for nearly two years; finally, he got a job teaching and saved enough to study in Paris, where he was revolted by what he saw; he returned home with an overwhelming urge to paint America.

Such a dramatized version of his life is often part of an artist-lecturer's stock in trade. It didn't seem a good idea to debunk himself, especially since the commonly accepted story was the peg on which the book was hung. But if he started to pin down details, as demanded by a book, it would appear that his father wasn't a Quaker, that his parents were less rigid and religious than the average and didn't oppose his drawing, that if artistic pursuits were subtracted he had never done much hard work, that he didn't build that ten-by-sixteen-foot shack but only fixed up Paul Hanson's shop, and that as far as the original idea for *American Gothic* was concerned he was revolted by what he saw in America—European Gothic was something he admired; this flimsy dwelling and these long faces were to be the "Gothic" America offered.

Writing was one of the least prosperous of Grant's sidelines. The few short published pieces bearing his name were written with some aid from faculty friends after he went to the university. They are in a general vein and in somewhat ornate style, not like the prose he wrote as a high-school teacher, not like the good-humored letters he wrote home, and not like the language he spoke. They don't have the feel of the man in them, and they don't contain much information.

The book dragged on for years. Its projected title was shortened from "Return from Bohemia" to simply "Return." It was going to be a book "to discourage imitators and sycophants." It was going to prove that art "can be dynamic and significant without violating esthetic principles." It was going to be representative "of the esthetic progress of every American painter of the period worth his salt." It would come out in the spring, in the fall, after the first of the year. But somehow it was never quite finished—it never came out at all.

THIRTY TWO

A Democratic Experiment

GRANT'S large public benefited him only indirectly when it came to the sale of paintings. Collectors were naturally influenced by the generally favorable reaction to his pictures, and this was the first factor in determining his status as an artist; but in the end a painting could have only one buyer, and that necessarily a person of some wealth, or a wealth-supported institution.

He wanted some way of getting a wider sale of his work. Ever since he had had the lithographing shop in the basement of the Green mansion at Stone City, he had been interested in this art. He didn't do anything with it then, but he kept it in mind and brought up the subject again four years later.

With other artists, he arranged to sell lithographs for five dollars apiece through Associated American Artists, Inc., of New York. In 1937, he made his first two lithographs, *Seed Time and Harvest* and *Tree Planting*, the former picturing corn ears hung out to dry on an old barn, the latter from the tree-planting scene which he hung in McKinley High School after selling *Arbor Day*.

His worktable for the lithographs was an old pulpit which he had picked up in an abandoned church. With his spectacles and squint and his close concentration, he looked a little like a nearsighted preacher deciphering fine print in a Bible. He worked with a special crayon to transfer his drawings onto lithographing stones.

Once a stone had been treated with chemicals and inked, around 250 lithographs, or occasionally as many as 500, could be run off in a press before the stone was ruined. Each copy was as original as any other, and each was to be signed by the artist himself. It was the nearest thing possible to mass production of original works.

This was the sort of thing his public could afford. While he worked over his pulpit, 250 copies of his first lithograph were sold before he could even complete it, and a good many more orders for it had to be refused. He had been nervous about how the first copies would turn out, but was satisfied with the result.

"I like the medium very much, and plan to do considerable work in it," he said. "It is a democratic experiment, like Currier and Ives."

His third lithograph was *January*, or *January Snow*, the most widely discussed of them all. Here he was back to corn shocks again but with a different treatment. Instead of straggling and brooding, these corn shocks had been bent by a strong wind into uniform shape, turned rigid by cold, encrusted and hooded with snow. They were arranged to speak with one voice of the silent desolation of open, inland country, where no oceans modify the terrible cold. The only relief was a row of rabbit tracks leading from a tepeelike opening in one of the shocks.

Even the purely esthetic were inclined to single out *January* as a powerful picture, though they could do without the tracks. The row of rabbit tracks was his usual touch of homespun realism, and something he happened to have on his mind at the time —the same rabbit tracks had recently crossed the snow behind the shanty in his drawing *Village Slums*.

From the bleak pitch of *January* Grant dropped to *Saturday Night Bath*, a painting that created a sensation in a limited circle because despite every effort he couldn't get it shown to the public. The picture showed a horse tank and a farmer beside it, taking a bath. The farmer had his head thrown back, pouring a bucket of water over himself, and was shown at full length, front view. Grant didn't follow the time-honored tradition of shrinking and shadowing the male parts. He invited more than fifty people to his house for the unveiling of the painting. It stood on a high rack over the sideboard, and both his dining room and living room were full of men and women that night. Strange to say, it was the men rather than the women who were embarrassed.

It might be thought that Grant intended this painting only for select gatherings, but such didn't seem to be the case. He crated it up, shipped it off to one of the country's major exhibits and sat back to wait for the sensation it would cause in the nation at large. Instead, he got a letter from the exhibitors "strongly recommending" that it be withdrawn. There was a certain muscular insistence behind this recommendation; Grant finally agreed to withhold the painting and to sell it privately. Its owner has never publicly revealed himself.

But Grant didn't give up. He still thought that in a less rarefied atmosphere than that provided by the exhibit halls it would be considered a very appealing scene. It was, in fact, nothing but stark realism. Grant insisted that all he had done was give artistic treatment to a homely operation which in his days on the farm had been quite common.

"In my boyhood no farms had tile and chromium bathrooms," he said. "After a long day in the fields, and after the chores were done, we used to go down to the horse tank with a pail. The sun would have taken the chill off the top layer of water; we would dip up pailsful and drench ourselves."

So he made a lithograph of *Saturday Night Bath,* or *Sultry Night* as it was later called. The postal inspectors looked at it and shook their heads; it couldn't get through the mails. Some copies of it were sold over the counter, and Grant gave others to friends. He always seemed puzzled by the fact that this picture had been barred from the mails.

Dr. Earl E. Harper was the newly appointed director of the university's school of fine arts and was interested in the chapel that Grant had planned for a site on the Iowa River, opposite the

Memorial Union. Dr. Harper was ready to start a fund-raising drive to get money for the building, but first he wanted Grant to sign a contract stipulating that he would do the murals depicting the development of religious life in Iowa. The chief reason for putting up a chapel was to provide space for these murals.

Grant demurred. He had begun to lose interest. If Dr. Harper had come along with his contract two years before, when Grant was making the mural designs, he wouldn't have had any trouble getting a signature. As it was, he pursued the subject for several months without getting a definite answer. Grant wasn't sure when he would be able to get to it, he would have to think it over, he wasn't sure he'd have the time.

He still avoided portrait painting, with a distaste that persisted year after year. This aversion disturbed his admirers, many of whom considered portraits his most important work. It seemed out of character, since he didn't usually tire of things. Yet there were definite periods in his painting, and when one of his phases had run its course he would turn from it with strong dislike.

That was what happened to his Gothic interest. When he painted *Stone City* and put a Gothic window near a corner of the Green mansion, it was quite out of place; the mansion wasn't that kind of architecture. But it was close to *American Gothic*; he had a feeling for Gothic windows, so he put it in. Then after *American Gothic* became famous, he never seemed to want Gothic windows anywhere, not even where they would have been appropriate. That was something finished and done.

The same thing happened to his Memling phase. *Portrait of Nan* really belongs at the end of his Memling period. Grant brought the portrait out later and gave it the date of 1933, but it was painted in 1931. It was entered in the 1931 Iowa State Fair and didn't win a prize—a bad piece of judging. After that Grant never wanted any part of Memling in his work again. He was persuaded to paint a portrait in 1933, *Portrait of Mrs. Donald Mac-*

Murray. It was a very good portrait, with a look of youthful expectancy, but it wasn't like his earlier portraits—he had left Memling. It was during the latter part of his stylized landscape period, and he put a few bulbous trees in the background.

In 1937, he had three portrait offers, two for ten thousand dollars each and one for seventy-five hundred. The offers came from wealthy eastern families attracted by his work. He found reasons for refusing them. He said he wouldn't paint a portrait unless he could see special character in the face, and after investigating one of the portrait possibilities reported: "There wasn't anything there; I couldn't do anything with it."

"You don't paint a portrait of a baby," he added. "It hasn't lived; there's nothing to tell. It may be a beautiful baby, but a camera would tell you that." At other times he would say: "It takes me so long to do a portrait, I can make more money with landscapes." Or he would say: "Usually the people with money to pay for a portrait are the very ones who have nothing to put into it."

He did accept one portrait commission in 1937—for considerably less money than the larger offers. It was to be of Charles Campbell, a pioneer banker at Kalamazoo, Michigan. Campbell's son-in-law Merrill Taylor had asked Grant to do the portrait, and Grant went to the Campbell home and stayed for a week. During that week, he gave no indication as to whether he would accept the commission but talked on general subjects and studied the banker's face. At the end of the week, he agreed to paint the banker in a golfing pose. But after more than a year of intermittent work on the portrait, he still wasn't satisfied with his drawing.

In the course of rejecting portraits, murals and federal jobs, Grant had plenty of time for remodeling and furnishing his house. That severe old Victorian residence, planted sideways in low ground with its five upstairs windows staring into the street, had stood there for years looking like a run-down college boarding place; now Iowa newspapers began rashly referring to it as "the most beautiful home in America."

Grant and Sara lived on the first floor. It was more than a year after they moved in before they considered the place furnished, and then Grant kept on making improvements. Visitors walked with anticipation past the drooping willow toward the entrance of the house. They stopped in the hall to examine a bin, opening like a flour bin and lined with galvanized iron, which he had made for rubbers and overshoes.

To the right was the downstairs bedroom, its floor covered with a foliage-green rug, its walls in white wallpaper with a design in big-stalked and big-leafed green vines climbing upward. Wardrobe closets and shoe drawers were concealed in the walls, and white corduroy curtains with a close-cropped green fringe were hung on three giant windows rising ten feet above the floor under a fourteen-foot ceiling.

Beside the bedroom was a tile bath done in vivid green, with peach-colored shower curtain and towels. Across the hall was a large rectangular living room: a reddish-brown carpet, more huge windows, more white corduroy curtains and more white wallpaper, this time with red flowers. A fireplace had to be built in; fireplaces were considered old fashioned in 1858. Bookshelves reaching to the ceiling surrounded a door to a side porch.

The side door had formerly hung on the inside. After building the bookshelves around it, Grant hung the door on the outside. With the thickness of the wall added to the thickness of the shelves, the door was recessed more than two feet. Over the fireplace he put *Portrait of Nan*, solemn, pensive, perhaps a little hurt and fearful, with the young chicken in her hand.

On a shelf running high around the dining room was arranged a set of century-old serving dishes, a present from William Allen White. The dishes looked down on a dining table, twenty feet long, big enough to feed threshers; fifteen or twenty dinner guests didn't crowd it.

An ancient clock, which had belonged to Grant's father and was dated 1854, sat on the dining-room mantel. On either side of it were Victorian bracket lamps which he had bought at the Amana colonies—a religious community established some ninety years before near Iowa City. Most of the second floor was converted into an apartment, in which Eric Knight, author of *This Above All*, lived for several months. Grant enclosed the yard with a low picket fence, set out trumpet vines, and restored the green shutters around the windows. Except for plumbing, heating and kitchen conveniences, he didn't make many concessions to modernism.

"Any further changes will be in the direction of restoration," he said. "Modernistic furnishings may be satisfactory for stores, novelty shops and hotels, but they are things of the moment with no tradition or future."

He still liked to economize on materials and to find uses for pieces of junk. There was a closet, under the stairway, that needed a light in front of it. No light could be put in the low ceiling above the door because the closet door opened even with the ceiling. So Grant sank a washbasin upside down into the ceiling and screwed a bulb into that. The enormous dining table looked to be walnut, but was actually made of a length of three-ply Masonite supported on iron feet taken from an old drugstore counter. The fireplace smoked, so he hammered a hood for it out of brass. He wanted a lounge chair "that doesn't rise up around me like an old-fashioned feather bed; a comfortable chair, yet not too soft," so he designed one with long armrests and deep-tufted seats, but no cushions. This was patented as "The Grant Wood Lounge Chair."

Relations with Cedar Rapids improved in the spring of 1938. David Turner, Marvin Cone, Arnold Pyle and others joined with the Cedar Rapids Art Association to put on a home-town exhibition of his works, mostly earlier paintings. Grant's only comment when the exhibit was being prepared was "Please don't dig too deeply," but he was obviously pleased.

He and Sara sometimes went on motoring tours in the country to look for subjects. Most of his lithographs were landscapes or were taken from outdoor subjects. The highway tours were the more sedate versions of the sketching trips he had formerly made up Indian Creek and along the Wapsipinicon.

Entertaining at their place continued. Grant was a convivial though somewhat retiring host. He had reached the point where he could drink five highballs before dinner with no visible effect other than an appetite, and then keep a glass in his hand most of the evening. He really preferred straight Scotch whisky.

He avoided as much as possible anything having to do with business or finances. His business affairs were in the hands of his agent, Reeves Lewenthal of the Associated American Artists, and Sara was in charge of their domestic finances.

"I don't have any money worries at all," he once told Paul Engle, the poet. "Sara takes care of everything."

THIRTY-THREE

"A Free Man Again"

THE winds blow very hot and very cold in Iowa. Twenty degrees below zero is common enough in the winter, and it's always five or ten degrees colder in the country. The snow hardens until farmers can walk up and over huge drifts to their barns. Then in summer, 100-, 105- and 110-degree heat drones over the cornfields.

Iowa houses are built for the weather. There's no shivering around on a chilly day, as in the south or even in California; when it gets chilly, you start a good fire in the furnace and keep it going as long as you need it. And when it's hot—well, there's not much you can do about that, but you have the satisfaction of knowing that the corn may grow six or eight inches on a hot day. Farmers feel so good that they drive into town for a beer or two and laugh heartily over anything resembling a joke.

Among the farmers around Iowa City, which like Cedar Rapids is in the black-soil belt, the name of Grant Wood was well known. For some reason farmers are generally noncommittal on almost every subject except the weather, and even there they hedge their predictions a good deal; but they would venture a "He's pretty good, I guess" if Grant's name came up, and their wives would rejoin: "Good! He's a great man; they won't know how good he is until after he's dead."

That was the firmly implanted conviction, that a man is never recognized until after he is dead, though it wasn't true at all in Grant's case. His success was recognized everywhere, and his students regarded him with respect. His was the only name on the art faculty that was known outside of artistic circles.

Yet his manner was self-deprecating and he still had a look of innocence. He always bowed slightly when he met someone he knew, always spoke with a smile and never seemed in a hurry. His studio was on Iowa Avenue, across the street and up the block from the five-cent hamburger hut. He usually walked the mile and a half from his home: he had been ill, his weight bothered him, and his doctor had ordered exercise; he also did stonecutting in his basement for exercise, and put in a large vegetable garden.

Overalls weren't quite the thing for the campus, but he still wore overalls when he worked around his place. "I'm a pretty good farmer; things grow pretty well for me," he liked to say. He grew sweet corn, tomatoes, cabbages, lettuce, radishes, beans, beets —the usual garden truck. He took great pride in his garden, and one day arrived at his next-door neighbor's with a basket of vegetables polished and arranged, looking as though they had come out of one of his pictures.

He was getting back to painting, starting where he had begun as a schoolboy, with water colors. In the spring of 1938, he painted two water-color dining-room pieces, one of fruits and the other of wild flowers—intricate work, the kind he had done with flowers brought over from the Turner funerals. There seemed no reason to doubt that he had created a solid new world for himself in the university setting.

But beneath the surface more than one thing was troubling him. After three years, his marriage was showing signs of severe strain. He was also disturbed and distressed over the failure of his teaching ideas to spread throughout the art department. He demanded that the students be given more chance to paint. A section of the faculty regarded him and his works with extreme distaste. He was convinced that a "vicious campaign of defamation" was in progress against him.

And his belief that he had no money troubles proved most ill founded. Internal Revenue employees often checked up on names that appeared in the newspapers. One day an agent put his finger on the name of Grant Wood, wrote it on a slip of paper and went to the files. What he found, or didn't find, surprised him. According to the newspaper, this man was living in "the most beautiful home in America," was the creator of perhaps $100,000 worth of paintings, and was paid hundreds of dollars for lectures, yet he had no income-tax report on file. No income-tax report for 1935 . . . no income-tax report for 1936 . . . and, deep in 1938, no income-tax report for 1937.

Two agents called on Grant for an explanation. He began to realize that his financial affairs were a cause for worry. Though the collector's office took a lenient view because he was an artist, and though university salaries at that time were exempt, he saw that it would take some complicated figuring to satisfy the government. He now had to face the fact that he was already heavily in debt. His income as it stood wasn't enough to cover his scale of living.

Under the university's plan of instruction, students began actual painting in the third year of the course. This was an improvement over the practice in many institutions, where a student could take a four-year art course without doing any painting at all, but it wasn't enough to suit Grant. As he put it, young fellows anxious to make a career of painting were kept grinding at the traditional subjects for two full years before beginning practical work.

Knowledge obtained from instructors and books was all right, but it was secondhand—and he didn't have much respect for the secondhand. A student got firsthand knowledge only when he himself was engaged in the work of creating a painting. He leaned toward the apprentice or disciple system of teaching. A student should work without any discordant voices or conflicting opinions ringing in his ears. And it was better when the professor, assuming he was a good one, showed the way by painting instead of talking.

He insisted that his students paint themselves into their pictures—their interpretations, their feelings, things from their own experience. One critic called it the fourth dimension in art: the depth of the artist himself. This dimension, along with narrative, characterization and information, Grant thought was overlooked by those who set up a goal of esthetic purity.

As had been the case at McKinley, he took his teaching seriously and was not inclined to compromise. When he thought his students were being confused by the teaching of theory, he carried protests to Dr. Harper who, as administrator, was trying as nearly as possible to satisfy both sides of the controversy. Such protests heightened the conflict between Grant and those who disagreed with him. There was also a personal side—jealousy, aversion to his lack of sophistication, and some of the dislike noticeable in almost any professional group for a man who deals directly with the public.

In the late summer of 1938, his marriage collapsed. Besides the friction caused by financial difficulties, there was a clash of personalities. Grant was slow and deferential in conversation; Sara was more outspoken. Grant was most at home with the simplest people; Sara liked a higher level of society. Through trying circumstances, Grant's role had been that of a mild and passive husband, but their differences mounted.

Finally they quarreled, at the dinner table. It was a serious quarrel. Sara left the table and went upstairs. Grant went out to mow the lawn. Sara's son Sherman came out to say that his mother was ill. Grant told Sherman to call an ambulance, and kept on mowing the lawn. The ambulance arrived. Grant kept on mowing. The ambulance took Sara to a hospital. Grant finished mowing the lawn.

The break came after a long series of events, and Grant was in no mood to make amends. "He is slow to anger, but he's got a memory like an elephant," Nan used to say, and John Reid echoed her: "He was very persistent in his hatreds." While his wife was in the hospital, Grant went to Clear Lake, in northern Iowa, where he was setting up a summer studio in an old railway depot. There he learned that she had returned from the hospital to their home. He telephoned Dr. George D. Stoddard, his best friend on the university faculty, and made it plain that he wanted her to be gone before he returned.

Sara left on a Saturday morning in her new Chevrolet. Grant returned the same day, in the afternoon. After that he kept bachelor quarters in the old Oakes place. The separation didn't cause a break between him and Sara's son, Sherman, who stayed on with Grant for several months.

A satisfactory settlement of income tax was reached, but he was left deeply in debt. His banker advised him to go into bankruptcy, but he refused.

He got the divorce a year later. The petition recited that he and Sara had lived together until September 17, 1938, and that the plaintiff "at all times conducted himself toward the defendant as a good and loving husband," and charged, in the usual legal language, that her conduct had been such as to injure his health. Notice was served on Sara in Orange County, California, but she didn't contest the action.

A settlement was reached before the decree. It granted her the 1938 Chevrolet sedan, two insurance policies with a net cash surrender value of $382 (above $521 in loans), an immediate payment of $117.69, and $5,000 in $125 monthly installments as long as she lived, provided she did not remarry. She was forbidden to use his name, on pain of losing the payments, and was restored her maiden name. He paid the attorney fees. She got all the books and furniture that had belonged to her mother, including six silver forks and other heirlooms; the rest of the property remained with Grant.

Even before the separation, Grant had been trying to recover the mood of Turner Alley—his old habits of steady work, of digging into his past for material, of spending months planning and months painting a picture. In 1935, Thomas Benton, impressed by the drawing for *Adolescence*, had written that if Grant didn't make a painting of this, he (Benton) would. Grant had assured him that he would paint it eventually, and was still thinking of it. The acclaim that had greeted the lithograph *January* created a demand for it in oil, and there were several other unfinished projects on his mind, including the Campbell portrait. In addition, he had new ideas for paintings.

Yet while planning a comeback, he didn't want anybody in Cedar Rapids to think that he was admitting to a mistake. The people there who had argued that an artist should paint and who had advised him against everything likely to interfere, including his marriage and moving from Cedar Rapids, were not to think he was suffering regrets. "I'm no torch-bearer," he said, "and I haven't given up painting."

Some of his backers were inclined to include teaching and lecturing as wearing distractions that kept the artist from his art, but Grant wasn't willing to give up anything in which he was established. Lithographing would continue. A leave of absence from teaching was the most he would consider. "I teach for what I can get out of it," he said. "No artist can afford to lose contact with life. These students are the changing generation; if great changes are coming, they will live through them. If I can maintain contact with the changing generation, I shall be able to change, too. That's the real reason I like teaching."

The only thing he ever said to Marvin Cone about the divorce was: "I'm a free man again."

THIRTY FOUR

Artist's Return

HIS painting comeback developed slowly. He continued to work in water colors through the rest of 1938, producing a total of four "dining-room pieces." Then he did lithographs in the same subjects as his water colors, *Fruits, Vegetables, Tame Flowers,* and *Wild Flowers,* and sent them to Nan for her to tint—his only colored lithographs. Nan, living in Los Angeles, was painting on glass, in a stylized manner, and had had a New York exhibition of her work earlier in 1938.

He did more black and white lithographs—*In the Spring, Fertility, Shrine Quartet, Honorary Degree, July 15.* In April, 1939, he had a minor operation. He asked for a list of everyone who had had anything to do with his hospital care, from the kitchen on up, and presented each with a lithograph. Back on his feet, he finished out the teaching year, and then really got back to painting in June. In three weeks he produced a set of twin landscapes, *New Road* and *Haying,* sold to Carol Sax of New York. It was the fastest painting he had done since he began producing major pictures, and, except for *Saturday Night Bath,* his first work in oil since *Spring Turning* in 1936.

This still wasn't the decisive comeback he was planning. The picture he had been mulling over in his mind for more than a year was *Parson Weems' Fable,* the story of George Washington and the cherry tree. Here was a painting with an appeal to his nature. As early as January of 1939 he had been making public statements about the picture, and after he got to it late in June he spent four months over the drawing.

There is no telling when Grant's interest in historical painting first developed, but it may have gone back to a day on the farm when his father came home with a copy of *Pictorial History of Mexico and the Mexican War*, a ponderous volume by John Frost LL.D., which was "embellished with five hundred engravings from designs of W. Croome and other distinguished artists." And his interest may have been turned toward the less frequently mentioned side of history, and toward George Washington in particular, by something that was among the family heirlooms— a brown blown-glass flask, hip-pocket size. His great-grandmother on the Wood side had been Hanna Hollingsworth, and the flask was inscribed: "This pocket flask belonged to Col. Hollingsworth of Virginia and was carried by him during the Revolutionary war. He was on General Washington's staff and said General Washington had drank from it several times."

Since he planned to treat the cherry-tree story as a fable invented by Parson Weems, the good parson himself ought to be in the picture. Grant had often been amused by the practice among colonial artists of having someone in the foreground of their paintings, either pointing to or holding back a curtain on the rest of the picture. In *Herbert Hoover's Birthplace* there was a small figure of a man, not very noticeable, pointing at the house. He planned to have Parson Weems in the foreground of the picture, holding back a curtain on the fable he had invented.

It would thus be apparent, upon closer examination, that what he was portraying had nothing to do with the real George Washington but only with a certain fable told by a certain Parson Weems. According to Parson Weems, what George Washington said exactly, when his father discovered the mutilated tree, was: "I can't tell a lie, Pa; you know I can't tell a lie. I did cut it with my hatchet." (It is usually rendered "little hatchet," but the word "little" was not in the parson's script.)

Grant's thought was that this was a very smug thing for a small boy to say. He didn't bother to explain his ideas much in the

223

statements he made before going to work on the picture, but said that George Washington would be portrayed as a very smug little boy. "He's going to be the smuggest darn little kid you ever saw," he said on one occasion, and on another: "George is going to be a real little six-year-old kid, and he's got to be smug."

Smug? George Washington smug? People were inclined to think that Grant Wood had gone out of his mind. You couldn't portray the father of his country offensively, not even at the age of six. Why, there'd be a hanging party out somewhere near the old Oakes place. Or he'd be ridden out of town on a rail. Indignation began to rise at the mere prospect of such a painting.

That was fine. It was as legitimate for a painter as for a writer to make capital of suspended interest. When *Parson Weems' Fable* appeared, people would look at it, and perhaps be indignant. Then they would look again and see that maybe there was something in what he said. At least they would see that Grant Wood was himself again.

Parson Weems was an itinerant preacher and book peddler who did a little winter preaching at a church called Pohick in Truro, Virginia. General Washington had attended that church, at a previous time, and there were those in the congregation who remembered him. Parson Weems gathered anecdotes and wrote a pamphlet, *The Life and Memorable Actions of George Washington,* on the cover of which he somewhat inaccurately described himself as "former rector of General Washington's parish." In the fifth edition of the pamphlet, the incident about the cherry tree was included for the first time.

The parson was a little vague about how this story came to him but very definite about what happened. He had Washington's father asking: "George, do you know who killed the beautiful little cherry tree yonder in the garden?" And then he had this to say about young George: "That was a tough question and George

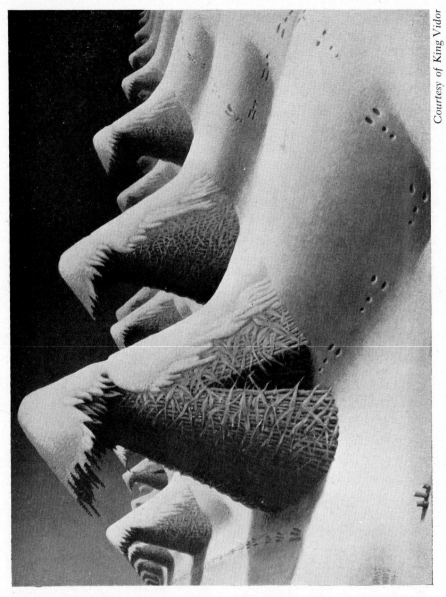

JANUARY

staggered under it for a moment; but quickly recovered himself; and looking at his father with the sweet face of youth brightened by the inexpressible charm of all-conquering truth, he bravely cried out, 'I can't tell a lie . . . etc.' "

The man who wrote so glowingly about truth was the man Grant planned to portray as one of the largest liars of all time. Upon further research, however, it developed that Parson Weems was no ordinary character. He had once had good Episcopal parishes in Maryland, and had got into trouble partly because of his sense of humor: sometimes even when he was praying the parson couldn't resist giving a humorous twist to what he said. He defended Tom Paine and "other infidels," denounced the slanders being spread against them, and held special services every other Friday for Negroes—a bold thing in his day. After he took to the road he almost flooded the country with pamphlets and books: one year he sold three thousand Bibles. In short, whatever might be said of his veracity, Parson Weems was a man of energy, courage, sympathy, feeling, humor and imagination. Grant gave him the most imposing place in *Parson Weems' Fable*; standing large in the foreground, holding back a rich red curtain with one hand and pointing with the other, he dominated the picture both in size and expression.

The deeper he got into Parson Weems the less importance Grant attached to the figure of Washington. His idea of portraying Washington as a smug little boy, except for what he could get into the posture, dwindled away. What he needed was something that everybody would immediately recognize as George Washington. He finally took the head from Gilbert Stuart's famous portrait of Washington—a full-grown head, the one everybody recognizes as that of the first president—and put it on the body of a six-year-old child.

This caused more gasps than any other aspect of the picture. There was George Washington at the age of six, with his wig and bow on and a face as mature as it ever got. Grant had already made his drawing for George Washington at the time he decided to switch to the Gilbert Stuart head, and the original for young George later was one of two designs which he furnished for ornamental goblets to the Steuben Glass Company.

Thus as the project developed, Parson Weems and his curtain took up almost half the picture. Washington's father was shown with his hand on a fallen cherry tree, and young George had his chest out, pointing at his hatchet. The design demanded that the cherry tree be perfectly spherical; it looked a little like a large green beach ball, studded with cherries and with a slender trunk attached. Grant finished the painting at his home rather than at his studio. Dinner guests came out. He ate with them and went back to his painting. "I can't get this tree . . . I can't get this tree," he would say. To make a cherry tree perfectly spherical and still have it look like a cherry tree was not an easy matter. Sometimes he would look at the picture and say: "This is really a mess."

By dint of some extraordinary effort—in one stretch he painted twenty-two hours without stopping—*Parson Weems' Fable* was completed and shipped to New York the day before Christmas in 1939. It was sold to J. P. Marquand the day after its arrival for seventy-five hundred dollars. One of the stipulations in the sale was that Grant would get 50 per cent of any resale profits, a measure suggested by the fact that he had seen *Daughters of Revolution* sell for four times what he was paid for it, and had seen others of his pictures multiply in value. The resale provision was new in America and attracted considerable attention.

"The idea is not new," said his agent, Reeves Lewenthal. "It has been discussed for years by liberal artists' groups, though so far as is known it has not before gone beyond the discussion stage in the United States. In France, however, the law grants artists part of the resale profits."

226

The reaction to the picture was violent in some quarters. Prints of it appeared everywhere; professional patriots and publishing colonels were outraged; indignant letters-to-the-editor were written. Grant was denounced as a man who had accepted money from the government, on PWAP, and then had proceeded to debunk the father of his country. But such things were on the surface; the more general attitude was one of tolerant interest and amusement.

Grant's position was that he liked the cherry-tree story and hoped it would continue to be taught—as a fable. Taking an optimistic view of the advances in education during his life, he said:

"When I was a boy we all learned the story of George Washington and the cherry tree, and accepted it as gospel truth. The present, more enlightened younger generation, however, is well aware that the incident never happened but was invented by Parson Weems.

"In making my interpretation," he added, "I have taken a tip from the parson and used my imagination freely—in an attempt to create an effective pictorial design and at the same time to tell the essentials of the story as the average person visualizes it."

If anything, Grant was more imaginative than the parson. Parson Weems boggled when it came to saying that the tree was cut down; he couldn't quite imagine such a muscular six-year-old; he only said that the tree was "barked" and "killed." But Grant showed the tree prone, almost cut in two, apparently by one masterful stroke. That it supposedly was February, the day after George's birthday, didn't prevent the cherries from being large and ripe; that it was 1738 didn't keep him from showing a modernized house.

Parson Weems, in his long, well-fitted coat, a little lean from his zeal, with a large, interested expression in his eyes and the smallest trace of a smile, got most of the newspaper space devoted to the picture. Some critics felt there was "an underhanded smile lurking somewhere in the canvas"; others thought the parson looked pleased at becoming known as the creator rather than the mere recorder of his story. They dug up anecdotes about him and recalled that he was quite a fellow in his day. Something better than the cherry-tree story—the parson's personality—was resurrected from the past.

Sabbatical Year

THE seventy-five hundred dollars Grant received for *Parson Weems' Fable* raised his income that year above twenty thousand dollars for the first time. He was in his sixth year at the university, and applied for a leave of absence during 1940–41. He had planned to follow with another historical work, turning the story of Pocahontas around to make it "Capt. John Smith's Rescue of Pocahontas," but he put it off. The first thing he did after *Parson Weems' Fable* was to go to Cedar Rapids and restore *Woman with Plants*.

The fact that the portrait of his mother has had to be restored and that its colors have darkened somewhat has not decreased its popularity; on the contrary the demand for it has risen every year. The phenomenon is not new in art: *Mona Lisa* had cracked and peeled, its red had turned to violet blue, its yellow had passed into green, and its blue had become a dull gray long before that portrait achieved its present enormous fame. Deterioration in surface and tone did not destroy the basic character of either picture.

Things were almost the same in Cedar Rapids as they had been before he left. His comeback was recognized; word went around that he was again the man who had painted in 5 Turner Alley; most of the friendships were renewed. He was back there often, in the role he liked best: that of a helpless genius—a role which was almost necessary for him because his mind simply refused to attach itself to the nonartistic details of living. He once went out to see Nan in Los Angeles. He forgot to tell her when he was coming, which didn't make much difference because he missed the train he was intending to take. He reached Los Angeles and got into a taxicab, but couldn't remember her address. He got out, sent a telegram to Cedar Rapids asking the address, and waited three hours for a reply. All this didn't bother him since the Los Angeles station is one of the nation's finest and as good a place as any to let the mind work out some of its unfinished business. But if it hadn't been for Park Rinard it is hard to imagine how he would have managed. "I always make three copies of everything," Park used to say. "One is for myself, one is for Grant, and one is for Grant to lose."

It may seem strange that a man holding a professorship could be painting at all hours and traveling and lecturing over the country at odd seasons. At the University of Iowa, Grant Wood was a special case. If he didn't appear for his classes, it simply meant he was somewhere else. Ordinarily, if any member of the fine-arts faculty wanted to leave town, Dr. Harper required a written statement of his reasons; when Grant left the city Dr. Harper only expected to be advised.

Grant would come to Dr. Harper's office and say he had to go on a business trip. He wouldn't say where he was going or why, and Dr. Harper wouldn't ask him. Grant would say that his students were well started in their work and could continue with what they were doing while he was gone. Would Dr. Harper look in on them now and then and see how they were getting along? Dr. Harper would.

In this way Grant again avoided any hard and fast routine. Yet his interest in teaching was intense, especially when he detected a glimmer of talent. He once heard that a young man of possible talent had been observed at work in the Amana colonies and he went down to investigate. The colonies, known as the Community of True Inspiration, had once opposed decoration, but were later liberalized, and John Noe had begun to do some painting there. Grant found Noe copying Gibson girls. He wasted no time but got

right to the point. "That's no way to paint," he said. He took Noe
to a hillside overlooking a bridge and they set up their easels.
"Now you and I are going to paint this bridge together," Grant
said. Young Noe, suddenly finding the state's foremost artist
descended on him as a teacher, could scarcely do less than he was
told.

So an artist was born in the Community of True Inspiration.
That Noe wasn't enrolled in the university made no difference to
Grant; he himself had been an unregistered and nonpaying stu-
dent at the school, and he gave Noe all the instruction he could.
David Turner was easily persuaded to buy a painting from Noe,
as he had done for any number of Grant Wood protégés.

Grant's students at the university were free to travel wherever
they liked, to paint murals or anything else for which they could
get commissions. He thought that if a student could make a little
money while he was learning to paint, it was all to the good; in
fact it was much better training when a student was painting for
money. He often had students as guests for dinner or an evening
at his house. He liked especially to have younger guests, and included among them the student correspondents for various newspapers around the state. Eddie Green, young managing editor of
the Iowa City paper and a friend of Park Rinard's, moved out to
live with them. Because of Grant's nearsightedness, his guests
sometimes got the impression that he was peering at them and
that he had a slight stoop. His smile has been described as
Buddhalike.

To the old Oakes place, too, came nearly every notable and
every artist who stopped in Iowa City. Almost without exception, they wanted to meet the painter of *American Gothic*. Iowa
City was a convenient stop on the Des Moines–Omaha–Denver
rail route, and visitors were frequent. In this way, and on his
travels, Grant came to know most of the leading artists of the
day. His own travels were extensive: in 1940, he was in New York

three times and in Los Angeles twice besides all the intervening
lecture stops.

The more he progressed in his painting comeback, the more
fierce became the feud between him and the other faculty members. His leave of absence from the university was granted and
passed as a routine matter, since it was his seventh or sabbatical
year, but it was doubtful if he would ever return. He wrote to John
Reid, still on the state board of education, that "my feelings in
this matter are too deep to discuss." He demanded a "thorough
housecleaning"—a step that meant getting rid of a good part of
the art faculty, and one too drastic for the university administrators to consider. When Grant began his leave of absence in 1940,
no solution of the dispute was in sight.

His health was far from good that year. He had gone on a diet
and had lost considerable weight. When he visited Los Angeles
on a lecture tour in February, he was so ill he could hardly stand.
Yet he carried through with his lecture tour, and did more work
in 1940 than he had done in any year since he left Turner Alley.
He first went to Kalamazoo and with the final coats of glaze completed *Portrait of Charles Campbell*, which he had started nearly
three years before.

It was a long way from the intensity of his Flemish portraits.
Campbell was shown looking out at a golf ball with an expression
of mild pleasure, tempered by age. As a rule Grant thought an action picture—"something in between this and that"—a very tiresome thing to look at, but he thought there was a place at the end
of a golf swing, before the club dropped, when the subject was
completely relaxed, and that was the pose he chose for Campbell.
He had had it in mind as a major picture, to be called "American
Golfer," but the Taylors and Campbells considered it a family
matter and asked that no prints be made. So it didn't become
well known.

Grant seemed bent on winding up things that had been hanging over him for years. He did the oil of *Adolescence*, a project which he had had just ahead of him for nine years. He painted *Oliver Wiswell*, from a drawing of that colonial character that he did for Kenneth Roberts' book by the same name. He had often spoken of wanting to do something with Henry Wallace, the public figure he most admired, and made a drawing of him that was used on the cover of *Time* magazine. And he painted the oil version of *January*, which had been in demand ever since he brought out the lithograph. The painting was sold to King Vidor.

Along with several other artists, Grant was taken to Hollywood in the summer of 1940 to paint scenes from Eugene O'Neill's *The Long Voyage Home*, which was being produced by Walter Wanger. The painting that resulted from this trip, *Sentimental Ballad*, was perhaps the most naturalistic thing he ever did: a print of it looked like a photograph from the movie. Actors John Qualen, John Wayne, Thomas Mitchell, Joseph Sawyer, David Hughes, Jack Pennick and Barry Fitzgerald were shown around a piano, singing and crying in their beer.

As his output of paintings increased, his lithographing fell off. In 1939 he had produced nine lithographs—*March*, *Shrine Quartet*, *Midnight Alarm*, *In the Spring*, *Fertility*, and the four, *Fruits*, *Vegetables*, *Tame Flowers*, and *Wild Flowers*, which Nan had spent four years coloring individually. In 1940 he added only one lithograph, *Approaching Storm*.

He did a poster for British war relief showing a woman and child crouched under an attacking plane. The America First Committee was then active, and asked him to do another poster favoring its campaign. Grant was among those who hoped that Roosevelt's policies would keep the country out of war, but he was not an isolationist. He refused to do anything for America First.

While painting and entertaining notables, he continued to find time for more homely pursuits. Sometimes he came walking across the lawn to play rummy with his nearest neighbor, John Oakes, a son of the builder of the Oakes place. Frequently he would call his physician, Dr. A. W. Bennett, and say: "This isn't professional, but could you come over?" If Dr. Bennett wasn't too busy he would stop in and talk for a while. Although on leave of absence during the winter of 1940–41, Grant attended many of the university social gatherings at the Jefferson Hotel and one night startled the management by ordering beer served, in bottles, at a formal dinner. His taste didn't run much to beer, but he seemed to think that a few plebeian bottles of beer was just what this formal gathering needed.

He took great pride in his exercise machine, which was contained in a cabinet, six feet high and four feet wide, with double, mirrored doors. Inside was what appeared to be a robot giant, made of wood and wires, with handles hanging down from its outstretched arms and its face severely turned away. Spring weights on pulleys issued from its arms, another spring weight came from its head, and handgrips for strengthening the finger muscles were fixed in its sides. There were dumbbells and Indian clubs, a chinning bar overhead, and a portable rowing machine, which Grant used more than anything else. He also kept up his stonecutting, chiefly for the exercise. He was planning a fish pool for his back yard, and spent an hour a day in his basement cutting half spheres in stone slabs which were to serve as the border. He built an enclosure of window shutters in his back yard, and took sun baths.

Everything he produced during his leave of absence sold almost immediately. Probably no artist ever got more publicity or had more collectors seeking his work. The drawings for his lithographs sold for from five hundred to a thousand dollars. Anything he put his name on was worth money. He had a polite remark which he made when visiting the studios of artists who had paintings that were waiting for buyers. "My, I envy you fellows who have your own pictures," he would say. But the envy was always on the other side.

If he hadn't worked so slowly, he would have made a fortune. As it was, he was constantly in debt. By the end of 1940, however, he had cleared up the worst of his debts; his assets almost equaled his liabilities. His financial recovery was the result of a group project: Grant produced the pictures, Harry Wade of the university kept his accounts and made out his income tax, Reeves Lewenthal handled his business affairs, and Park Rinard managed the house.

Early in 1941, in the grip of winter, he did two more lithographs, *December Afternoon* and *February*. The seasons of late were providing him with most of his material. He said he was tired of satire and would do no more of it. He was as persistent as ever in doing only what he wanted to do, and it was one of his convictions that nothing else could be good. Just now his carryover projects were completed, and he was working on fresh ideas for paintings.

Spring in Iowa

SPRING in Iowa was never better than in 1941. The cottonwood and box elder and slippery elm never leafed out sooner; the iris buds never were fatter; the plum trees, spendthrift and overeager, never blossomed earlier or sent more of their fragrance drifting over the hills. Uncertain winds from the south explored their way northward, doors were left open, and blades of grass straightened their backs.

Grant, leaner than he had ever been, wearing a short-sleeved sports shirt, was at work in his Iowa City studio, on *Spring in Town*. Here was a picture of things at the beginning, warmed by an indulgent sun. There were nine figures in the picture, and he always made separate drawings of each of his figures; they were thumbtacked above him as he bent over his main sketch.

He had fully regained his old habits of work. *Spring in Town* grew from the smallest and surest details he could find close at hand. George Devine, son of football coach Glenn Devine, posed for the central figure—a man with his back turned, spading in a garden—and the house in the foreground is an Iowa City house. The rest of the picture was made up from odds and ends gathered to fit the composition.

Iris buds beginning to open, as they usually are when you're spading . . . those foolish plum trees, putting forth blossoms before getting their leaves . . . dumpy, ill-lighted, angular houses, man's handiwork standing out starkly against the softness of nature . . . that nonsensical screen door again, with more fretwork than ever . . . someone climbing a ladder to fix a loose shingle . . . mowing the lawn . . . rug beating . . . a child going past with a coaster wagon . . . blankets with familiar designs, being hung out to air . . . a birdhouse such as he put up in Kenwood. It was from such blocks that the painting was built.

Things weren't so peaceful out in the world. War feeling in the country was steadily rising. England had weathered the blitz; Hitler was preparing his attack on Russia; American war materials were being shipped in increasing quantities. There were people who thought an artist could be better engaged than in painting something about spring in town. Grant said:

"We have everything we need to meet any threat. Our chief weakness, as the president has pointed out, is that we're going about our defense effort halfheartedly—that we aren't really awake to what we stand to lose. Here, it seems to me, is where the artist comes in.

"This isn't the time for smart, sophisticated stuff in any of the arts. On the other hand, I think the other extreme of flag-waving is just as bad. Artists should go on painting simple, everyday things that make life significant to the average person."

He did nothing more with "Capt. John Smith's Rescue of Pocahontas." Like most of his other series, *Parson Weems' Fable* remained a series of one. Alongside *Spring in Town* he worked now and then on a sketch for *Spring in the Country*, a landscape done in moderate curves. "I'm not going to become a bitter old artist; I'll quit painting first," he said. He was fifty years old; he had been away from teaching for a year and had put a good number of paintings behind him; he was interested in getting a settlement of his university dispute.

John Reid was working on the matter. Reid had the double task of getting all the concessions he could, and then persuading Grant to accept them. Reeves Lewenthal flew out from New York, fearing a blowup that would damage Grant's painting and lecturing prestige. Such a blowup seemed possible, with Grant campaigning against the university administration if he didn't get what he wanted.

The position of the university administrators was difficult. There was the school's academic standing to think about. Grant represented the controversial present, and there was more safety in the settled matters of tradition. To conservative university people, having Grant Wood at the head of the art department, and Grant Woods of assorted sizes on the faculty, would have seemed like going native in a very brash way.

On the other hand the public was ready to back Grant Wood. If he was the best artist on the staff, the only one in fact who could be said to have produced a lasting work, why shouldn't he be head of the department? Or at the least, as he demanded, why shouldn't his ideas be put into practice? As is well known, one of the principal functions of a state university president is to get appropriations from a state legislature. Legislators are rude fellows, who often side with the public—not as often, perhaps, as might be desired; still, they have an ear to the ground.

A compromise was indicated, and was finally arranged. Grant, appointed an associate professor, was raised to a full professor of fine arts. This meant more prestige, though his salary remained at thirty-six hundred. More important, he was separated entirely from the art department. Four skylighted studio rooms were set aside for the exclusive use of him and his students. He was cut off from contact with his late antagonists on the art faculty; he was a separate entity in the school of fine arts. Students didn't register for his course in the art department; they registered through Dr. Harper's office.

That was the arrangement that had been agreed upon when Grant, pursued by hot weather, left for Clear Lake and his last summer in northern Iowa. He was in his best painting form; reluctant as he had been to compromise his university demands, he was glad that matters were settled. He finished *Spring in Town* and began painting *Spring in the Country*. The Cedar Rapids paper again reported small details of his movements, and Cedar Rapids people often came to see him.

Clear Lake is a small resort city, where popcorn is sold on the street corners and every third house has a "Tourist Rooms" sign. The lake is much like the Minnesota glacial lakes. Grant's studio was in what had been a small-town railroad depot, originally moved up there to serve as a summer cottage. It was placed among some small apple trees, about ten yards off federal highway No. 18 on the west edge of the city. The hum and roar of passing cars and trucks didn't seem to bother him.

A foundation of cement blocks had been put under the depot, raising it about four feet off the ground. There was no front step; he had to hoist himself into it. It was like getting into a boxcar. The door opened on what had been a baggage room, now musty and piled with boards and boxes. A path led through them to the studio itself—a long, narrow room, its windows covered with cloth to keep out insects. On one side were two long benches and on the other a table for paints, bottles of oil and paint remover, a radio, discarded sketches and trash. There was a bucket with a dipper for drinking water and a granite basin for washing the hands.

It looked to Cedar Rapids people like something he might have fixed up before he went to the university. On the walls were figures of stick-men and animals and such inscriptions as "Yours till Hell freezes over and the Devil goes skating." He did this kind of thing when he was concentrating on something else. The shadows of discontented insects could be seen crawling around the edges of the cloths at the windows, and occasionally a June bug power-dived into one of them. Sparrows nested under the eaves, and these, the least musical birds ever to become vocal, kept up a constant yeep-yeeping outside.

Unfinished, *Spring in the Country* stood on a tall easel. The bucket and dipper, being handy, got into the picture, but he didn't like the way the bucket was placed. In an effort to determine what was wrong, he had Park Rinard stand beside the bucket, as the woman stands with her hoe beside the bucket in the painting. He eyed Park up and down, and studied the bucket. Then he got a compass and measured the distance between a plumb line and the bucket, first on his sketch and then on the painting. He always insisted that a compass was more accurate than inspiration. He finally decided that by dropping the bottom of the bucket a trifle he could make it look all right.

A neighboring farmer was called in to examine the painting. He withheld judgment on the picture as a whole, but he gave Grant a certain approval: "I see that you've got the shadows under the cows." That comment pleased Grant. The cows in the picture were at a considerable distance, in a pasture beyond the plowed land, and it didn't seem to make much difference whether or not the shadows were shown. This particular farmer, however, felt reassured by their presence, and might have noticed something missing if they hadn't been there.

Grant had a cottage a half mile from the studio on the edge of the lake. It was a two-story house, with a south-screened porch and a long series of steps leading down to the dock. He walked to and from the cottage for lunch, kept up his exercises with dumbbells and spring weights, took sun baths on the dock and sometimes went rowing, in a rowboat that for some reason was named "Tobacco Road." He still liked to swim, but had to give that up because it affected his sinuses.

The cottage was furnished with pine furniture and some favorite lounging chairs. There was a shelfful of books. On the floor near one of the chairs lay a copy of William L. Shirer's *Berlin Diary*, read to about page 88 and tossed into a corner—Shirer also grew up in Cedar Rapids. To John Reid, who visited him at this time, Grant seemed in better spirits than he had been for years. He was relaxed, good-humored and full of ideas for pictures.

He liked to walk through the town in the evening and stand on street corners at about the time darkness was beginning to set in.

He finished *Spring in the Country*, which was sold to Cornelius Vanderbilt Whitney, Jr. *Spring in Town* was sold to the Sheldon Swope Art Gallery of Terre Haute, Indiana.

When the late-afternoon shadows began to stretch out over the lake, Grant went back to Iowa City and directed the furnishing of his studios. He designed boxes that hooked into the wall casements to hold paints and brushes, while the students worked on the walls themselves. In this realm of his own, he seemed about to start on a new and quieter period of teaching.

It may have been too much to expect the university to come around to his way of thinking. The emphasis on the classical heritage and the recognized masters of the past was bound to seem to him a poor way to solve the everyday problems of painting, but it was what was to be found at every other school. In fact Iowa was unusually progressive in the matter of practical work. Perhaps a colony like Stone City was more suited to his ideas; perhaps Dave Turner had been right years before when he had asked, "Why teach?"

Grant at any rate seemed reconciled to spreading his ideas only as he could teach them himself, in a small circle within a circle. And he was determined to paint more steadily than he had in his other teaching years. He was planning another one-man exhibition in New York for 1942, and had an idea for a new and more serious series of historical paintings.

He taught three weeks under the new arrangement. Then he went to Dr. Harper's office and said he had to go on a business trip. He had made a short trip to the south early in 1941, but his main lecturing tour that year had been postponed. Now he went on a tour that took him to Florida and up along the east coast.

His health was not good. He attended the dinners and after-

lecture sessions to which speakers are invited, and seemed determined to get around as usual, but there was no spring in his
movements and he refused drinks with the explanation: "I haven't
been well."

Back in Iowa City, he did what was to be his last lithograph,
Family Doctor—a study of Dr. Bennett's hands holding a stetho-
scope and a thermometer, with a watch lying on the table. It was
in a far different mood from that of his other study of a doctor's
hands, *General Practitioner*, the *Main Street* illustration. Then
he had in mind the inefficiency common enough among medical
graduates; now he was trying to pay tribute to the medical profession.

Summer had long since given up the ground it had won. The
first wet snows had fallen, and an icy chill had bitten into the
soil. Some people wouldn't want to live in such sharp changes of
seasons, yet how by contrast they emphasize each other! A few
months ago this ground was alive with spring; now the cornstalks
were drooping, with hard, dry ears of corn clenched in their husks,
and the landscape was withered, like a receding face in a dream.

Grant stayed on at the old Oakes place for two weeks after he
returned from his tour. His last visitors at home included Arnold
Blanch, Adolph Dehn, Doris Lee and Yasuo Kuniyoshi. These
were fellow artists who regularly stopped at his place when they
traveled west. His health continued to grow worse. He had a diges-
tive pain; he thought he was suffering from gallstones. Exercise
and dieting didn't seem to help. Dr. Bennett decided to turn him
over to specialists at the University Hospital.

He entered the hospital on November 24, 1941. No one knew
what was wrong with him. The doctors decided they would have
to perform an exploratory operation. Grant agreed to it on one
condition: that they tell him what they found. It was set for
December 19. On December 18, he made a one-paragraph will,
leaving everything to Nan.

The operation didn't take long. The doctors had hardly made their incision before they saw it was cancer, in an advanced stage. They called it cancer of the liver, but it was a secondary invasion of the liver—the growth had been present in other organs. Its removal could not even be thought of; there was no hope.

THIRTY-SEVEN

Last Days

GRANT was told two days later, before Nan could get there from California. Park Rinard, who knew, waited outside while the doctors were with him, and came in as soon as the doctors left. If anyone could have been welcome at such a time, it would have been this friend and secretary of the last seven years. But Grant asked to be alone, and explained: "I've just received some news that requires a readjustment in my thinking."

A few hours later when Park looked in, Grant said: "It's okay; you can come in now; everything's under control."

What he thought during those first hours he never said. Naturally his mind had explored every corner of this prison that had closed about him, and had found no escape. There was no escape to be found.

Yet he thought he detected a crevice. After all, the doctors didn't know how fast this thing would develop. One of his long-standing convictions about himself was: "The last thing I do always seems to be my best." He might still have time to do some painting.

"I want to get back to my studio," he told Dr. Harper. "I've still got a lot of pictures I want to paint."

Word passed among his friends that he was dying. They came down from Cedar Rapids for their last visits, and Grant was glad to see everybody who came. He was especially warm toward Dave Turner. He heard that Dave was making up a huge scrapbook of clippings and other mementos of their friendship, and insisted that the book be brought to the hospital for him to sign. The scrapbook was big enough to cover the top of a desk, but Dave

244

carried it up to the room the next time he came. Grant wrote in an uneven hand: "To Dave Turner with my best regards. Grant Wood." During these last days, they were as close as they ever had been when Grant was living at 5 Turner Alley.

Grant thought that after the effects of the exploratory operation had worn off, he would get stronger for a short time. When three weeks had passed, however, it became apparent that it was not the aftermath of the operation that was keeping him at the hospital. He decided he ought to resign from the university. He called Dr. Harper to the hospital and handed him a sealed envelope.

"I'm doing the thing I think I ought to do," Grant said. "I hope you will do as you think best with this."

When he got back to his office, Dr. Harper opened the envelope and read the short resignation which said that Grant would probably be unable to continue with his teaching during the coming semester, and that in justice to his students he felt he should withdraw in order that other arrangements could be made for his classes.

A day or two later, Dr. Harper went back to the hospital and told Grant his resignation had been rejected. Grant was pleased. He was never more genuinely pleased in his life. He was desperately anxious to maintain his connection with the university at the last.

He reached the point where he didn't want to leave the hospital under any circumstances. Yet it worried him that perhaps he shouldn't be there. The hospital was crowded, and what could they do for him?

"Do you think it is all right if I stay here?" he asked Miss Prescott.

Miss Prescott couldn't imagine what he meant. She said of course it was all right.

"Do you think it is being selfish?"

245

"It's just whatever you want."

"I could go home. But I have a rather bad time of it about four o'clock in the morning. I want to be here, where there are nurses and doctors."

This was almost too much for Miss Prescott. She assured him again, "No, no, Grant, it's only what you *want* that matters," and found reason to hurry from the room.

Twice during January, he had to borrow money, on notes at an Iowa City bank. The first was for $1,600 and the second for $900. These brought his liabilities, including the mortgage against the house and bills of all kinds, to $23,679. His assets as they were valued afterward came to $21,159.

When he gave up the idea of leaving the hospital, he clung to the belief that he could still do some work. He signed his last lithographs; he talked over the telephone about his classes; he examined and graded paintings which his students brought over; he passed on a master's thesis. He thought there would be days when he would be up and around the room, and could do a little painting. He told Marvin Cone: "I'm going to paint right here in the hospital. Park's going to bring my paints over in just a few days."

In these last days he seemed to feel that *Woman with Plants* was his most enduring work. He decided to paint a portrait of his father. It would be a companion piece to *Woman with Plants*. He told Marvin he was sure he could do it, even though he was only ten when his father died.

"I've got an old daguerreotype of him," he said. "And I remember him—I remember him well."

He knew he was not leaving much of an estate. For Park Rinard, there would be the manuscript on which they had worked together so long. This last painting of their father was to be for Nan.

Robert E. Neff, the hospital administrator, heard of his plan and arranged to set up a studio in the hospital. As soon as Grant showed any signs of being able to paint, Neff planned to vacate a room on the same floor and have someone in to see that it was right for an artist.

Neff never had to go to the trouble; Grant didn't get any stronger. He was so weak that he couldn't hold up an ordinary book long enough to read it. After visitors left, he slept until about midnight, then woke up and read ferociously until four or five in the morning—usually twenty-five-cent, paper-bound detective stories. A larger book which he wanted to read was cut into three sections for him.

He could hardly have missed in the faces of his visitors the fact that they knew he was sinking, but he tried to keep the conversations on a bold level. He spoke of his illness as though it were temporary, and of the time when he would be back on his feet again. "Come on now, cheer up," he kept saying to Nan, who had lived all her life looking up to her brother and didn't find it easy to smile or banter.

Thomas Benton called on him late in January. Grant winked as Benton came in the door. Only the previous spring he had visited Benton in Kansas City and had said: "Tommy, I think you may see something really good come out of me in the next few years." Now he talked again about getting back to painting, though he knew there was no longer any hope, not even for a single brush stroke. He was gaunt, his skin was yellow, his abdomen distended.

Miss Prescott and the Stoddards visited him the Thursday before he died. They didn't think they ought to stay. They stood at the foot of the bed and talked for a while. Grant asked them to sit down, but they edged toward the door. Finally Grant said: "I'm going to be hurt if you don't sit down."

They sat down. In a feeble way, Grant was delighted.

"You know," he said, "the doctors say I can have a little stimulant at this time of the afternoon. I think we'll have a party."

He raised himself on one elbow and poured himself a small glass of whisky from the stand. He held it under his nose and moved it from side to side, as he always did in his later years to get the full flavor of it, and drank it down.

Then he talked of his students and the promise they had shown. And he told of a dream he had had, in which he was carrying an enormous pane of glass, so big and so heavy that he couldn't set it down. No one was around to help him, and he walked and walked, without ever seeming to arrive anywhere. He laughed heartily over this.

When Miss Prescott and the Stoddards left, Park Rinard was waiting in the hall.

"That's goodbye," he said. "You won't see him again."

Preparations for the funeral were begun. Dave Turner received a telephone call from Park Rinard, who asked him to go to Anamosa and buy a cemetery lot.

"What do you want to *buy* a lot for?"

"It's on account of that damn lion."

Dave Turner said "oh." He drove to Riverside Cemetery in Anamosa. There were the Wood and the Weaver family lots, side by side. Plenty of room for Grant in either of them. The rest of the cemetery was beginning to get crowded. Why not put Grant in the Weaver lot, next to his mother? Dave drove back to Cedar Rapids and wrote to Park Rinard: "If you feel that it is absolutely necessary to purchase a lot in another part of the cemetery, to get away from the lion, I will be glad to take you and Nan to the cemetery. But it does seem that inasmuch as there is room next to his mother in the Weaver lot it would be best to use the space."

It was agreed that the Weaver lot would do. Grant died at

10:00 P. M. on Thursday, February 12, 1942, two hours before his fifty-first birthday. He was heavily drugged for the last three days. The last coherent word his night nurse heard him say was "Nan." Both Frank and Nan were at his bedside.

His estate wasn't hard to figure up. It included only two completed paintings—*Currants*, the water color he had done in 1907, and *Spotted Man*. There was an unfinished portrait of himself that he had started in oil from the 1932 drawing, and there were several sketches, including his last: a landscape showing frostbitten corn shocks and barren fall trees that he had done just before entering the hospital. The house and furnishings, salary and insurance due, some interest in drawings and lithographs on consignment—that was about all.

Members of the university faculty issued memorial statements. Dr. Stoddard said: "Grant Wood painted what he knew . . . and sometimes he had a little fun." The funeral was held on Saturday, in the Turner chapel, with his paintings looking down and with the light from his pastel-colored window softening the shadows. There were plenty of flowers—more flowers than Dave Turner knew what to do with. Two hundred and fifty persons crowded into the chapel. Poems were recited and hymns sung.

Then the funeral cortege wound north and east over the highway, past Stone City, past Waubeek. Grant went back for the last time to the Wapsipinicon valley.

Up in Riverside Cemetery the lion still sleeps over the Wood graves. Grant's grave is scarcely half a dozen good steps from the lion, but the lot where he is buried is marked by another stone, a masterpiece of rectangular simplicity, with small oak leaves in the corners and WEAVER spelled out in large strong letters. On the grave itself is only a small headstone: GRANT WOOD 1891–1942. There is no place for an epitaph. If an epitaph were needed, Dave Turner thought of one as good as any when he filled out the standard burial papers required by the state. After puzzling what to put after "How long was deceased employed by above company?" Dave wrote:

ART WAS HIS LIFELONG PROFESSION

Important Paintings by Grant Wood

TITLE	YEAR	OWNER
Currants	1907	Mrs. Nan Wood Graham, Los Angeles
The Dutchman's	1916	David Turner, Cedar Rapids
Feeding the Chickens	1917	David Turner, Cedar Rapids
The Horse Trader's	1917	David Turner, Cedar Rapids
The Old Sexton's Place	1919	David Turner, Cedar Rapids
Looking for Wigglers	1919	David Turner, Cedar Rapids
Misty Day—Paris	1920	David Turner, Cedar Rapids
Fountain of Voltaire	1920	David Turner, Cedar Rapids
Square at Chatenay	1920	David Turner, Cedar Rapids
Round House, Paris	1920	David Turner, Cedar Rapids
Gardens, Versailles	1920	David Turner, Cedar Rapids
The Cow Path	1922	David Turner, Cedar Rapids
Portrait of Vida Hanson	1922	Wayne King, Chicago
Italian Farmyard	1924	David Turner, Cedar Rapids
The Blue Door	1924	David Turner, Cedar Rapids
Fountain of the Medici	1924	David Turner, Cedar Rapids
Spotted Man	1924	Mrs. Nan Wood Graham, Los Angeles
Cottage, Brittany	1925	Mrs. Grace Crager, Cedar Rapids
Cherry-Burrell Workers' Portraits	1925	Cherry-Burrell Company, Cedar Rapids
Grandma's Place	1926	Frank Wood, Waterloo, Iowa
Old Shoes	1926	David Turner, Cedar Rapids
Autumn	1926	Gordon Fennell, Cedar Rapids

IMPORTANT PAINTINGS BY GRANT WOOD

TITLE	YEAR	OWNER
Church Door, St. Emilion	1927	Van Vechten Shaffer, Cedar Rapids
Roman Arch	1927	David Turner, Cedar Rapids
Door at the Foot of the Stairs —Perigueux	1927	Cedar Rapids Art Association
Quilts	1928	Jay Sigmund estate, Cedar Rapids
Midsummer	1928	Dr. Arthur Erskine, Cedar Rapids
Red Bedding	1928	Dr. Wellwood Nesbit, Madison, Wis.
Calendulas	1928	James L. Cooper, Cedar Rapids
Sunflower	1928	Miss Grace Shields, Cedar Rapids
Black Barn	1928	Arnold Pyle, Cedar Rapids
Yellow House, Munich	1929	Roland Moehlmann, Cedar Rapids
John B. Turner—Pioneer	1929	David Turner, Cedar Rapids
Woman with Plants	1929	Cedar Rapids Art Association
Portrait of Mary Van Vechten Shaffer	1929	Van Vechten Shaffer, Cedar Rapids
Portrait of Susan Angevine Shaffer	1929	Van Vechten Shaffer, Cedar Rapids
Arnold Comes of Age	1930	Nebraska Art Association, Lincoln
Stone City	1930	Society of Liberal Arts, Joslyn Memorial, Omaha, Neb.
American Gothic	1930	Friends of American Art, Chicago Art Institute
Overmantel Decoration	1930	Herbert Stamats, Cedar Rapids
Midnight Ride of Paul Revere	1931	Mrs. C. M. Gooch, Memphis, Tenn.

IMPORTANT PAINTINGS BY GRANT WOOD

TITLE	YEAR	OWNER
The Appraisal	1931	Dubuque (Ia.) Art Association
Portrait of Nan	1931	Mrs. Nan Wood Graham, Los Angeles
Portrait of Melvin Blumberg	1931	Michael Blumberg, Clinton, Iowa
Victorian Survival	1931	Dubuque (Ia.) Art Association
Birthplace of Herbert Hoover	1931	Gardner Cowles, Jr., Des Moines
Young Corn	1931	Woodrow Wilson High School, Cedar Rapids
Fall Plowing	1931	Marshall Field III, New York
Daughters of Revolution	1932	Edward G. Robinson, Beverly Hills
Arbor Day	1932	King Vidor, Beverly Hills
Spring Landscape	1932	G. Stewart Holmes, Cedar Rapids
Fruits of Iowa (five mural hangings)	1932	Montrose Hotel, Cedar Rapids
Tree Planting	1933	McKinley High School, Cedar Rapids
Near Sundown	1933	George Cukor, West Hollywood
Palmer Handwriting Series (five)	1933	A. N. Palmer Co., Cedar Rapids
Portrait of Mrs. Donald MacMurray	1933	Donald MacMurray, Chicago
Dinner for Threshers	1934	George M. Moffett, Queenstown, Md.
When Tillage Begins, Other Arts Follow (murals)	1934	Iowa State College Library, Ames
Death on Ridge Road	1934	Cole Porter, New York

253

IMPORTANT PAINTINGS BY GRANT WOOD

TITLE	YEAR	OWNER
Spring Turning	1936	Jo Hennessey, Bomoseen, Vt.
Sultry Night	1936	Anonymous
New Road	1939	Irwin Strasburger, White Plains, N.Y.
Haying	1939	Irwin Strasburger, White Plains, N.Y.
Parson Weems' Fable	1939	J. P. Marquand, New York
Portrait of Charles Campbell	1940	Merrill Taylor, Kalamazoo, Mich.
Adolescence	1940	Abbott Laboratories, North Chicago
Oliver Wiswell	1940	Kenneth Roberts, Kennebunkport, Me.
Sentimental Ballad	1940	Walter Wanger, Beverly Hills
January	1940	King Vidor, Beverly Hills
Self-Portrait (unfinished)		Mrs. Nan Wood Graham, Los Angeles
Spring in Town	1941	Sheldon Swope Art Gallery, Terre Haute, Ind.
Spring in the Country	1941	Cornelius Vanderbilt Whitney, New York

Index

255

INDEX

INDEX

257

INDEX

INDEX